PRAISE FOR
ORIENTATION TO GRADUATION

"The kind of book that makes you wish you could go back and do college all over again. Filled with insights (and humor) that really matter."

MICHAEL ZULAUF, graduate of UNC-Wilmington, entrepreneur, and teacher.

"A first-hand document that gives students and families insight into the realities of college life and how to use each moment to make an impact in the college community, build friendships, enlarge a network, and enjoy one of the most memorable times in life!"

TONI BLOUNT, Coordinator of College Advising and Scholarship

"Oh, my"...this is an excellent read for anybody looking forward to their first year in college, and for those already navigating the process of being a successful and happy student. Austin Helms combines natural enthusiasm and an entrepreneurial eye for the issues that really matter with an excellent, easy read. I can't wait to share this with the young folk in my family who are starting college next summer. "

DAVE BOND, International Leadership Facilitator, Executive Coach and Retreat Leader (Offices in South Africa, Europe and the USA.)

Orientation to Graduation is an excellent book which will be of practical help to students, teachers, and college bound families. I think this book should be required reading for every higher education faculty member who works with first-year students. You will learn things from students that you never would have thought of asking. It shows close attention to the ways today's college students live and learn. I will definitely plan on using this book with my future freshmen. The chapters on academic life and making the most of your social life are particularly useful, and offer a plethora of insights into making the most of a four-year college education.

DR. ANDY DIGH, Director of First-year Integrative Seminar, Mercer University

---

"*Orientation to Graduation* is a must read for any senior in high school, naturally experiencing that raw anxiety of leaving home and entering a brand new chapter of their lives. For that matter, O2G should be on every college freshman's bookshelf within handy reach for the friendship and support they will need!

MARILOU McFARLANE, SVP Global Business Development, Shotzoom Software.

"Austin discusses everything in this book from goal setting to social anxieties to college drinking and provides not only his experiences with all of this, but his unique perspective as well. I highly recommend this book to anyone thinking about going to college or currently enrolled in college as it will be as relatable as it is insightful."

DR. TIFFANY M REISS, Clinical Associate Professor, Washington State University

---

Helms provides an insightful and highly personalized account of the day-to-day struggles and triumphs of being a college student in his new book "Orientation to Graduation." His humorous and often heartwarming anecdotes prove that college can be both a fun-filled and a lesson-learning experience. With universally helpful advice in almost every aspect of college life, this guide is capable of motivating students of all strengths, interests, and beliefs to strive to take full advantage (or, as Helms puts it, "Make the Most") of the four short years of college.

ALEXANDRIA ANDREWS, current college student

"For new college students, Helms' earnest and thoughtful book will help them gain a set of fundamental skills to make the most of this new experience in their lives."

JUDITH CONE, Vice Chancellor for Innovation,
Entrepreneurship and Economic Development at
The University of North Carolina at Chapel Hill

Austin is the ultimate college tour guide. I would recommend this book to any rising college freshman. So much has been written about getting into college, Austin provides a first-hand look into life once a student arrives. Austin's friendly and honest advice provides just the tonic one needs to make the most out of the college experience.

CHRIS NG CASHIN, MBA University of Chicago,
Entrepreneur, and Father of Four

"The book brings a realistic perspective for young adults who think they are ready to take on the world, but one mishap could bring all those dreams to an end."

DR. LARRY PUTNAM, Superintendent

"Having worked with admissions and speaking to thousands of perspective students and parents during my time in college, I see *Orientation to Graduation* as a must have for any high school graduate heading to college. *O2G* gives advice and an inside look at the massive life changes that face students as they begin the next chapter of their lives in college."

RUSS RUSSELL, Texas Christian University '16

"*Orientation to Graduation* captures so much of the college experience, but is easily and infinitely readable, witty, comprehensive and spot-on with some excellent advice for every college student from small, private college to giant, sprawling public university. Helms offers up his own experiences as emblematic of the college experience, and he does so with great humor and without missing a detail."

DR. TIM FLOOD, Associate Professor of Management & Corporate Communication, UNC Kenan-Flagler Business School

ORIENTATION TO GRADUATION

ORIENTATION to GRADUATION

STORIES & ADVICE
— FROM A —
REAL
COLLEGE STUDENT

AUSTIN HELMS

Oh My Publishing
3229 Hollyhill Circle
Valdese, NC 28690
www.austinhelms.org

Ordering Information:
Quantity sales. Special discounts are available on quantity purchases by schools, school districts, corporations, and others. For details, contact the publisher at the address above.

Orders by U.S. trade bookstores and wholesalers. Please contact Austin Helms: Tel: (828) 448-5521

Printed in the United States of America

ISBN-13: 978-1545463550
ISBN-10: 1545463557

First Edition

Cover and interior design by Stewart A. Williams

Dedication

I would like to dedicate this book to my hero, Aunt Tina. Tina was an inspiration in every way. She was the happiest person I knew and lived everyday like it was her first. For eight straight years my aunt fought breast, bone, and liver cancer and finally found the cure on August 8, 2012. Tina now resides in heaven, where I know she keeps a close eye on me. I decided to dedicate this book to Tina because she always wanted to write a book, but she was busy fighting for her family. Just to show you how special Tina was, here are some quotes that she lived her life by:

"When nothing is going right, it's good to have someone on your left."

"Life isn't about waiting for the storm to pass . . . it's learning to dance in the rain."

"I would want God to say to me: you have been a blessing to someone else."

"Peace is a long hot bath."

"I love you more than dirt."

I love you, Tina.
Austin

TABLE OF CONTENTS

FOREWORD XIV

INTRODUCTION XVI

Part 1

Make the Most of Yourself

— 1 —

1. GOAL SETTING 3

2. FINANCES. 7

3. FOOD IN COLLEGE 10

4. EXERCISE AND SLEEP 13

5. FAITH 16

6. SUPPORT TEAM. 20

7. MENTAL HEALTH 23

Part 2

Make the Most of Your Academic Life

— 27 —

8. CHOOSING A MAJOR 29

9. TIME MANAGEMENT 33

10. EXAMS AND FINALS WEEK 37

11. BOOKS. 40

12. STUDY HABITS. 43

13. GRADES 47

14. PROFESSORS 51

15. STUDY ABROAD 54

Part 3

Make the Most of Your Social Life

— 61 —

16. ROOMMATES AND HOUSING 65
17. RELATIONSHIPS AND HOOKUPS 69
18. PARTY SCENE 75
19. INTRAMURALS AND CLUBS 81
20. SPORTING EVENTS 85
21. GREEK LIFE 88

Part 4

Make the Most of Your Opportunities

— 91 —

22. ENTREPRENEURSHIP OR ENTREPREDOERSHIP 94
23. NETWORKING 99
24. INTERVIEWS 103
25. INTERNSHIPS 109
26. JOBS 114
27. SERVICE 120
28. TRAVEL AND EXPERIENCES 124
29. MISTAKES AND FAILURES 128
30. MAKE THE MOST 133

FINAL THOUGHTS 135
AUSTIN'S TOP 16 LIST 139
ACKNOWLEDGEMENTS 141
ABOUT THE AUTHOR 142

FOREWORD

I have known Austin the entire time he's been writing this book, so with your permission I'd like to introduce him to you.

Austin's got roots. If his accent doesn't tell you where he's from, then he will. But what does that mean, "he's got roots?" It means he knows he came from a small town in western North Carolina, and that there's a huge world out there that he's eager to explore. But every time he steps out to explore, he carries his hometown with him, being as kind and as genuine to every new person and experience he encounters; as he would stopping to talk to a buddy while driving down Main Street in Valdese.

Austin's got goals. A lot of people you meet will tell you they dream of going on vacation in exotic places, or writing life changing novels. The difference between them and Austin, and hopefully you too, is that he thinks about what he wants for a while, then writes it down on a list and makes it happen. He's had a list of "Goals for Success" in his room for over four years, and he works toward them every day, rain or shine. More than that, for each one he crosses off, he adds two more. Much like his mouth when he gets to talking, he doesn't stop, and he doesn't let many things stop him.

Austin lives for the "oh my" moment. At some point around senior year, he started saying "oh my" a lot. Whether it was Brice Johnson yamming on somebody in the Dean Dome, a friend delivering the perfect zinger, or sitting in Kenan Stadium on graduation day in a sea of Carolina Blue, "oh my" was more than a catch phrase, it was his way of saying, "Wow, life's so big and full of surprises and I'm in one of those moments that truly make life worth living."

As someone who's been lucky to call Austin one of his best buddies, I think these three things pretty much sum him up, and I hope they will help you to better understand the man who's story you're about to read.

Now, unlike Austin, I tend to run out of things to say, and that's right about now. Besides, you bought this to read his story, so go on now, and enjoy. I know I'm looking forward to reading it too.

—*Mitch Dare*

INTRODUCTION

"ANYTHING IS POSSIBLE."

On June 18, 1994, a legend was born. Not really, just a kid from Valdese, North Carolina, named Austin Helms. My parents, Art and Amy Helms, are the reason why I even had the opportunity to write this book. My parents gave my sister, Anna Helms Lowman, and me the foundation to dream big and encourage us through every life stage—yes, even the middle school days.

Valdese, North Carolina, is a small town of 4,500 strong, where Friday nights rule all, and most folks have never even heard its name. However, Valdese is like any other small town in the United States; it's home to a high school full of students eager to graduate and attend college.

When I graduated from Jimmy C. Draughn High School in 2012, I was an "eager beaver," which I assume most of you are if you are reading my book. I was so ready for college that I couldn't stand it. I was ready to see the world, ready for an adventure, and ready to see my true potential! I packed my belongings and was ready to move in two months before my move-in date. While I was anxiously awaiting college, I had the bright idea to begin writing about my feelings and experiences via blogging, so I could one day publish a book based on my college journey.

It is important to note that this book was written by a real college student, in real time, with real experiences from orientation to graduation. I wrote this book for college students and future college students who not only want to **Make the Most** of their college experience, but also to help prepare students for what's after college.

It is also important to note that this book is written from my experiences: I am a proud graduate of the University of North Carolina at Chapel Hill; I am a Christian; my family was very involved with my college career; and I do things a little differently than most. However, this book can benefit anyone, and it's my hope that you can take some of my tips and advice and use them for your college experience.

College (in most circumstances) is the most challenging, yet rewarding experience of your young life. College allows you to step out of your comfort zone (if you make yourself do so), introduces you to people with different ideas, and helps you find your passions. It allows you to mess up, and mess up a lot. It's a clean slate. It doesn't matter where you come from, private, public, or home school, rich or poor —it's a fresh start.

College is special. It's a four-year journey that shapes you into the person you are going to become. The only person in control of your decisions, is you. You have to get up early, you have to study, you have to eat healthy, you have to say yes or no, and you have to make your own goals. College is tough, but it's so sweet.

I don't define college like this to scare you, but to prepare you for what's coming. It's just different. It's a place where you truly find yourself without your parents holding your hand. Trust me, college is fun, and anything is possible!

However, you have to keep in mind that in order to keep a well-balanced college life, you must **Make the Most** of every second.

PART 1

MAKE THE MOST OF YOURSELF

"IT'S ALL ABOUT BALANCE."

have never been able to roller skate. I used to be petrified of my local skating rink, the Pavilion. I was so scared of the Pavilion that when my friends would have birthday parties there I would cry my eyes out. I would then beg my parents for a few extra dollars to play in the arcade so I wouldn't have to skate.

Balance on the rink has never been my friend; however, balance in college is essential if you want to be successful.

In the following chapters, you will see what I think it takes to **Make the Most of Yourself** during college and topics that are relevant to living a balanced life:

Goal Setting
Goal setting is crucial even before you make it to college.

Finances
College is for anyone who wants to go,
no matter your financial situation.

Food
Food in college opens more doors to meet new people!

Exercise and Sleep
The Freshman 15 sounds scary. What is it?

Faith
We all come from different religious backgrounds, and I will talk about my faith in a way that will be helpful to all.

Support Team
People are the most important part of your journey.

Mental Health
Don't get discouraged. Take care of your mind as well as your body.

Before I left for college my mom reminded me, "It's all about balance, Austin. It's all about balance."

CHAPTER 1

GOAL SETTING

"DREAM BIG"

Everyone has goals. You may not know you do, and you may even be scared of them. But goals are powerful. When set the right way, they can stare you in the face, push you to new limits, disappoint you, and empower you all in the same day.

Before attending college, or if you are reading this during college, I want you to follow these simple steps. Even if you have defined goals in your head, this is a great exercise to brainstorm new goals for the next chapter of your life!

1. **Give yourself some alone time**. Find a place to be alone, maybe outside, on a beach, or maybe in the comfort of your own home. P.S. Bring a pen and a pad.
2. **Write down activities, hobbies, anything that you enjoy**. This can be anything from running/playing a sport to volunteering and helping people in need. Write down as many items as you can, in all areas of your life. I break it down into these four categories: Family,

Financial, Fitness, and Faith. For instance, I enjoy spending time with my family on vacations (family), starting businesses (financial), playing tennis (fitness), and going to church (faith).

3. **Write down what you enjoy about those things**. For example, running could either be a stress reliever or you could enjoy competing.

4. **Then write down things you would like to do**. This could be anything, really—dream BIG! These are your new goals.

5. **Break your desires into categories**. After you have created a long list of items, try and break those into categories. My 4 F's (Family, Financial, Fitness, and Faith) are just an example of a way to divide the categories. Some other categories could be travel, relationships, or academic.

6. **Make sure that you are really dreaming, and dreaming big with detail**. If you want to "travel the world," make sure you list the countries you would like to go to, and when you would like to visit them. Giving yourself a deadline helps push you to those goals.

7. **Print your goals and hang them on your wall**. When I first made a goal list at seventeen (senior year of high school), I only had a list of about fifteen goals, all of which were very broad, things like, "Find the love of my life." OK, Austin, easier said than done. During the spring of my senior year of high school, I printed my goals and hung them on my wall, where they still hang. Print your goals out and hang them somewhere that you will see them every day. By printing goals out, you make them real to yourself, real to your friends, and real to your family. When people know what your goals are, they are more likely to encourage you to reach them.

8. **Turn your dreams into a reality**. Make a plan to achieve your goals and go after them. Most times it takes small goals to reach the bigger dreams you might have. Be patient, believe in yourself, and never stop making your dreams a reality.

I have encouraged some of my friends to set goals and to make them real by printing them out. I'm not sure if any of them listened to me, but I am here to tell you that goal setting works, and has worked for me in so many instances. The biggest goal I set for myself when I started college was to get into the Kenan-Flagler Business School.

Choosing a college can be a hard task, and the decision truly comes down to a lot of factors. For some the academia can rule all, others might be more interested in extracurricular activities, such as programs, fraternities/sororities, or athletics. One of the main reasons that UNC-Chapel Hill was an attractive choice for me was their prestigious business school, the Kenan-Flagler Business School (KFBS). The undergraduate business program isn't something that you get into right when you start. It's a separate application process following your first year.

After deciding to attend UNC-Chapel Hill, I wrote my goal: "Be accepted into the Kenan-Flagler Business School." As I stepped on the campus in August 2012, I began my pursuit to become a student of the KFBS.

Goals are really fun to set, and to say, "Oh, I want to do this, and I want to do that." However, I have seen through experience that very few folks have the "doer" attitude. Most have the "talker" attitude; they just like to talk about doing things. If you plan on writing the goal down on your list, I challenge you to do it, whatever it takes.

For a list of my goals, check out my website: austinhelms.org. Also, if you feel extra motivated, send me your goals. I would love to feature them on my site!

For almost two years, I stared at "Be accepted into Kenan-Flagler Business School" on my goal list. The day of admission was on January 15, 2014, and it felt like the longest day of my life. The business school had informed us that the admission decision would be available on the fifteenth, but never specified a time. So, I waited, along with hundreds of other students. Finally, at 4:18 p.m., "We are delighted to offer you admission . . ." was all I needed to send me into a whirlwind of excitement. As soon as I heard, I called my parents, friends, relatives, past teachers, and maybe even people that didn't care. I had reached a milestone.

I share with you a success story of my goal-setting adventures to prove that goal setting truly does work. But trust me that with every goal set and completed, there are many more that fail. Goals continually change. Your goals might be changing as you read this book, and that's perfectly fine. They are meant to change, they are meant to push you, and yeah, sometimes they upset you.

CHAPTER 2

FINANCES

"YOU WON'T REGRET IT."

A ccording to the College Board, the average cost for tuition and fees for a four-year university in the United States was roughly $34,000 for the 2016–2017 academic year. College can be really, really expensive, especially if your family doesn't have the financial means to pay for you to go to college. I'm from a middle-income household, so I have lived the grind of finding financial aid, applying for scholarships, and taking loans that I am currently paying back. This chapter will outline how you can **Make the Most of Yourself** by keeping your finances in check.

I. **Apply, Apply, Apply:** Before getting to college, I applied for at least twenty scholarships that were offered at my high school, regionally, and at the national level. These applications involved essays, videos, and some even required interviews. I would encourage you to apply to as many of these scholarships as you can because the worst these committees can say is "no." Also, you can apply for scholarships each year; don't stop looking and applying just because you've been accepted to a school. Out of the twenty plus scholarships I applied for, I received three, which was helpful, but my parents and I still needed more assistance.

2. **FASFA (Free Application for Federal Student Aid):** Another to-do before you get to college! On January 1st of each year, FASFA allows students to apply for federal scholarships, grants, and loans. Before you even get to college, you will need to fill these free forms out if you would like to be considered for federal aid. "Better do your FASFA," my mom would always remind me on New Year's Day.

   This is by far the best way for you to get funding for your education. I have some friends who received full-ride scholarships, others who were awarded small grants, and still some who were offered loans. FASFAs aid comes in various forms, all of which are helpful and useful. In certain instances, FASFA can guarantee you money as a work study, which guarantees you a job on campus.

3. **Consult with you parents or guardians.** My dad loved to claim UNC-Chapel Hill as "his school," too, because he sent checks to the university on my behalf. I was fortunate to have my parents involved with my college career, and they were able to help support me financially. This doesn't mean that my parents paid for all of my school. I still have student loans to pay off, and I received numerous grants/scholarships during my time in college.

With that being said, if it wasn't for my parents, college would've been very different. I am not saying that I wouldn't have gone to college, but I would've spent more time working to pay for school. Some of you might be in the situation where you will have to pay for all of your schooling. Don't be discouraged. Instead, accept the challenge. College would've been doable without my parents, but would have definitely looked a little different for me.

At age seven I became an entrepreneur. To be more clear, I became a "shoebox entrepreneur." During my sister's basketball games, I sold candy to any fan that would pay me a whoppin' twenty-five cents for a mini-sized candy bar. I will explain my entrepreneurial story in a later chapter, but at the age of sixteen I started a bubble gum machine business. One Quarter at a Time began with one small bubble gum machine (the one that accepts quarters) and eventually spread to twenty-three machines. These machines fueled my activities in high school and went on to fund some of the fun things I got to experience in college.

I tell you this story to encourage you that no matter your financial background, you can make "One Quarter at a Time" and fund extracurricular activities you may want to experience in college. Finding a way to make extra money will allow you to experience more incredible things that college has to offer.

It may be hard to fathom, but no matter your financial background, you can **Make the Most** of your college experience. It will take perseverance, grit, and determination, but I promise you won't regret going to college!

CHAPTER 3

FOOD IN COLLEGE

"IS IT JUST ME, OR ARE YOU GETTING HUNGRY?"

ood. We all have to have it, we all enjoy it, and we all hate it when it makes us gain weight. Meals can offer you the opportunity to meet new people and give you a platform to try new things. Most colleges and universities now have offerings that appeal to all folks: those with allergies, vegetarians, gluten-free, you name it!

The college you attend will determine the quality and variety of the food offered. During my experience, the dining halls did a great job of offering a vast array of selections, providing enjoyable food, and hosting themed nights that gave students a taste of foods from other cultures. Food on college campuses isn't what I would consider fine dining, but it filled my belly with the proper nutrients I needed.

Here are my tips on how to take advantage of food on a college campus:

1. **Eat slowly.** During my time in college, I was always in a rush, so I ate quickly, not realizing the negative impact this had on my body and my mind. I quickly learned to slow down, enjoy my food, and whatever "it" is, it can wait.

2. **Eat lunch with different people.** This was one of my favorite things to do in college. Meeting new people and then grabbing lunch with them allows you to get to know someone on a deeper level, and also increases your network. My friends used to joke with me and call me "Mr. Networker." It wasn't that I was always trying to network, but I just really enjoy the company of others, especially people I don't know. Step out of your comfort zone and get lunch with someone new!

3. **Try new foods.** Hailing from Valdese, North Carolina, my diet didn't see much diversity, but when I arrived at UNC-Chapel Hill, my eyes were opened to all types of new foods. For instance, my first week I had duck, and during a study-abroad trip, I had the opportunity to try intestines. As I stated before, most colleges have options for all kinds of food preferences, and some even will cater to you if you have special food requests.

   Keep in mind, trying new foods allows you to become a more rounded eater. College can create a trap for bad eating habits. Don't get stuck eating fast foods. Branch out and try something new.

4. **Meal plans can be confusing—switch it up.** I understand that meal plans are different at each college, but they have some similarities. You will have the option of either getting: an unlimited plan, some kind of weekly plan, or in some instances, a block-style meal plan (ex. 160 meals/semester). In my opinion, I wouldn't

go with the unlimited plan. Unlimited plans can limit you to one food option, which in most cases is the main cafeterias. I was usually pleased with the food I received in dining halls, but I realize that everyone's taste buds are different. However, you might grow tired of the kind of food they make. I recommend either the weekly or block-style meal plans. These meal plans allow you to have more flexibility in your food options. The unlimited plan can prove to be costly, and limits how you spend your excess money. Switch it up!

When I gave campus tours, I would explain the dining experience like this: There are two types of dining experiences on campus, the buffet style and the mall food court. For example, most colleges/universities have some kind of cafeteria that offers pizza, burgers, sandwiches, different meat options, vegetarian options, and a salad bar. This is the buffet type of atmosphere. There are also other chain restaurants, such as Subway, Chick-fil-A, and Wendy's that offer food on campus, which might feel more like a mall food court. Keep in mind that universities will use different names for their meal plans.

5. **Eat Breakfast.** In my opinion this is the most important tip. If you hate breakfast, learn to love it and learn to eat it every day. Eating breakfast before a big exam is crucial! Nobody wants to have a grumbling stomach while you're writing an exam response. Breakfast is also another meal where others can join you!

I will say this a million times over in this book, but you really have to **Make the Most** of each second you have in college. The simple task of eating can open so many doors.

CHAPTER 4

EXERCISE AND SLEEP

"WHAT IS THE FRESHMAN 15?"

The Freshman 15 can become a harsh reality for students who don't have the proper amount of exercise and sleep. It is real and can be scary if you're health conscious. This phenomenon is caused by a number of things, such as limited sleep, bad eating habits, and lack of exercise. However, I hope to help you in the fight against the Freshman 15, which I was able to combat pretty well.

The Freshman 15 comes from drinking alcohol and partying all the time. FALSE! Don't get confused, if you come to college and plan to party hard and drink a lot of alcohol, you will gain weight, it's inevitable. However, there are plenty of students who come to college and don't drink a sip of alcohol, yet still gain that Freshman 15.

Think about it this way:

In college, you take three steps and you've made it to your mini-fridge, three more and you're in bed, and ten steps will get you to the bathroom. If you think about your home, you take many more steps than that getting to those locations. Add on the stress of homework, social life, and much more, it can all take a serious toll on your health.

Although college creates an environment that makes it easy to create unhealthy habits, it also creates an environment that allows you to create healthy habits. Students are surrounded by activities, resources, and intramural sports that encourage exercise. During my time in college, I found great pride in playing intramurals, running on outdoor trails, and trying new sports, like ultimate frisbee.

I would highly encourage you to devote at least five days per week to some kind of activity, and no, I'm not talking about walking to class as one of those activities. College has a physical activity for everyone. By staying active you not only help prevent weight gain, but can open your mind to new things, allow for more opportunities to meet new friends, and relieve stress.

One example of how physical activity opened my eyes happened during one of my runs through campus. While I was running something inspiring popped into my head. The thought was that each step I took was taking me one step closer to my future. I know that might sound a bit weird, but sometimes during college, the simple act of running or being active can change your perspective. So, keeping your body active not only helps you maintain body weight, but also gives you some new, positive outlooks on life.

Sleep works right alongside exercise in college. If you do enough of it, you will reap the benefits, but if you don't, you will see a dramatic decrease in your efficiency in the classroom and beyond. Too often, students will pull an all-nighter and cram for an exam. This is not only bad for your health, but it is also proven that this isn't the best way to study. I will talk about better practices when it comes to studying in a later chapter, but for now, please note that an all-nighter is not worth it!

MAXIMIZE YOUR SLEEP & EXERCISE

- Exercise five times a week for at least thirty minutes. This can be any form of exercise, and finding an exercise/activity that you truly enjoy is a way to make this much easier.
- Get involved with intramurals. Even if you're not an avid player of the sport, intramurals are an avenue that is for all levels of skill. During my time in college, I made some of my best friends playing intramurals.
- A combination of alcohol, lack of sleep, eating quickly, and little exercise can make that fear of The Freshman 15 become a reality. Stay away from those things. And if you don't heed this advice, exercise more!
- Never pull an all-nighter. Most exams in college won't come as a surprise, so plan ahead.
- Nap! Power naps are the absolute best and can help you tremendously if you're feeling stressed.

CHAPTER 5

FAITH

"IF YOU SQUEEZE A LEMON, PEAR JUICE SHOULDN'T COME OUT."

Faith is trusting in someone or something no matter the outcome. Faith can create a positive attitude and totally change your outlook on life. I am a believer in Jesus Christ. I believe that everything happens for His reason, in His timing, and sometimes you have to learn to dance in the rain. My faith wasn't always the strongest, but college challenged me and made me into a better person.

College is diverse; it's diverse in almost every way possible. College brings students together of all colors, all backgrounds, and from all faiths. With worshipers of different faiths coming together, there are times when students of differing beliefs might confront each other and/or learn something new about a faith that they didn't understand before.

Growing up a Christian, I went to church with my family, went to bible school every summer, and read the Bible on occasion. However, when I got to college, my parents were no longer there to make me go to church, there were way more distractions, and for the first time, I had to figure out what I truly believed. I can't speak to students of other faiths, but for some reason coming to college scared me because I thought I would lose my faith.

No matter your belief and no matter your upbringing, your faith will be challenged in college. It is my opinion that you should keep an open mind, listen to others, and listen to yourself. What do you truly believe? Why do you believe you are here? What kind of decisions should you make?

College will challenge your faith in many ways, and during my senior year, I was challenged more times than I can count. I was challenged with partying and drinking too much, how I was spending my time, and the way I was treating people. It wasn't until I was invited to church by my hair stylist that I began to see things clearly.

Debbie invited my friends and me to her church, The Church of the Apostolic Revival in Durham, North Carolina, and it turned out to be one of the most unique, meaningful church services that I had ever experienced.

The Church of the Apostolic Revival is primarily an African American church located in an old warehouse building. It didn't look or feel like a church until the service began.

The service started with singing from the children's choir, followed by the adult choir, and then came Apostle John, who delivered the sermon. The sermon was louder than any church service that I had ever been to, and was much different than the small-town church I was accustomed to attending. Although the preaching was loud, and we all left with a slight ring in our ears, the speaker was spot-on. I was able to see that no matter where you are, no matter what your sanctuary looks like, or your circumstances, you can live out your faith.

Following the service, my friends and I reflected on the experience, and really enjoyed some of the words of wisdom that Apostle John laid on us:

"I might be weak, but don't mean I'm sleep."

*"The key of persistence will open
the door of resistance."*

My all-time favorite line from the sermon was "If you squeeze a lemon, pear juice shouldn't come out." When I heard that, some things about myself became clearer. I was claiming to all of my friends that I was a Christian, but at the same time I was going out and doing non-Christian things. If you would've squeezed me during my senior year, lots of pear juice would've come out. I realize that nobody is perfect and we all make mistakes. However, I urge you to hold strong to your faith while in college. Temptations only produce short-term happiness.

COLLEGE WILL CHALLENGE YOUR
FAITH IN MANY WAYS

Other People

Every single person that you interact with in college will come from a different background. You will interact with Christians, Muslims, Buddhists, Jews, atheists, and all kinds of folks from different religious backgrounds. College is diverse because of this, which makes it so special. College accepts anyone and everyone, no matter their background.

Failures

I will talk about my failures in more depth in another chapter, but failure happens frequently. Failures can knock you down and make you feel worthless. Bad grades, not getting accepted into something you really wanted, and broken relationships are just a few examples of what your time at college can present you with. Just remember to hold true to your faith and things will get better.

Limited Time

Time management is an entirely different topic, but you will quickly learn that there isn't enough time in the day to do everything you want to do in college. There are papers to write, people to meet, places to go, games to play, faith to strengthen, etc. Find time for what you deem important, and you will find satisfaction.

I understand that I probably painted a really weird picture in your mind—a lemon with pear juice—it just doesn't make sense. In a lot of ways, college throws different things at you at the same time. There were many instances that I became overwhelmed with school, extracurricular activities, and temptations. I became someone I wasn't because of all of these pressures, and I became that weird fruit that didn't really make sense. However, my faith kept me on track, and my faith helped remind me who I really was.

CHAPTER 6

SUPPORT TEAM

"WE ALL NEED A SHOULDER TO LEAN ON."

We all need cheerleaders, we all need friends, and we all need supportive people in our lives. In my opinion, people are the greatest gift on this Earth. People are special, people are kind, and people show us the good in this world. When looking back on my college career, people are what I will miss the most.

One of the main members of my support team is my Granny Kat. I actually started a tradition during college where I would end the school year by staying with her for a few days. She lives at the beach, makes the best homemade biscuits, and likes to tell jokes. Granny Kat is a cool granny; it never really took convincing to visit her.

Granny Kat was a nurse for over forty years, and with that comes a lot of knowledge and experiences. She has witnessed births, deaths, and things I don't even want to imagine. Since my granny has this wealth of life experiences, I enjoy visiting her. I love to listen to her stories and ask her for advice. Being the person she is, she once left me with these tips:

"Wear socks when it's cold."
"Plant your garden in the ground."
"Don't take wooden nickels."

But after she gave that piece of knowledge about the wooden nickels, she couldn't remember why she told me that, so we let it be.

Your support group can give you a good laugh and make you feel loved.

HOW TO BUILD AND MAINTAIN A SUPPORT TEAM

I don't consider a support team as just your parents, loved ones, or family. I consider it all people that you come in contact with. I believe each person you meet in college can have an impact on your collegiate career. For instance, one of the first guys I met in school, Nick Kramer, gave me the opportunity to visit his family in London, which was the first time I had ever left the country. A support team comes in all shapes and sizes.

1. **Don't be scared to share your story or meet others.** When you first get to college, you will meet so many new faces. This was one of my biggest concerns when going to college—I literally thought I wouldn't make friends. However, within the first few days, I had so many I couldn't remember their names.

2. **Follow up!** Whomever you might meet, a future employer, a professor, a potential date, you name it, get their contact info and follow up. Following up means

sending a text, email, or handwritten note that alludes to future conversation.

3. **Learn to lean, support others, and have fun.** A support team consists of your friends, family, and mentors. You'll need to learn to lean on your support during times of troubles and stress. When I was struggling with something in college, I always knew I had someone to call and talk to about what was going on in my life. Don't be afraid to ask someone for help if you really need it!

    As you will ask others for help, they will ask you. Learn to say yes and to give back when your friends need help or assistance. You will learn quickly that the more likely you are to help someone else, the more likely people will be to help you!

While in college, I set out to visit a lot of my friends' hometowns. This allowed me to fuel two of my passions: travel and building relationships. Also, my friends' parents were always the nicest people, so that made it very easy. These travels allowed me to try world-famous barbecue in Lexington, North Carolina, hike to the Hollywood sign, see Big Ben in London, and to experience so many more awesome things that wouldn't have been possible without the friendships I had made.

I urge you to **Make the Most** of friendships during your time in college because you never know where they might lead you!

CHAPTER 7

MENTAL HEALTH

"IF IT WAS EASY, EVERYONE WOULD DO IT."

Overwhelmed, stressed, tired, and lonely are all things I felt while in college. They were real and sometimes they felt like they would never go away. I would classify my mental health in college as strong, but I still endured times where I felt like I wanted to pack my bags and go home. Mental health is a serious issue in college, and it's something that can't be overlooked. In order to **Make the Most** of yourself, you must keep a check on all parts of your life.

There are plenty of things that can cause a college student to have doubts, feelings of loneliness, or no motivation. These can be triggered by lots of issues that I have already mentioned, including lack of sleep, balance, support, and patience. When these issues bottle up, they can become scary for a college student. For example, my mental health hit a low point during my first semester freshman year, when I began to feel homesick.

Every college student learns to deal with homesickness in a different way, but I wish I was given at least some suggestions before experiencing it. Sometimes the college life can get very lonely, and it can make you want to give up. I have never been one to throw in the towel, but there were times that I considered giving up during my first year. Please note that homesickness is just a short-lived issue, and it will come and go. Once you learn how to combat it, you will be just fine. It will pass!

Before I left for college, my dad gave me a great piece of advice. He said, "Austin, college is going to be hard. If it was easy, everyone would do it." I took that advice to heart. It gave me motivation on a daily basis because it encouraged me to do my best even when the subjects or situations became difficult. His advice not only pertains to school work; the entire college experience can feel overwhelming and difficult at times. Whenever I began to feel down, I kept repeating his advice in my head. The more I thought about it, the more I began to smile because I realized I shouldn't have been dwelling on things I couldn't control; I should have been working hard because that is how I would become successful.

Again, it comes back to having goals. If you can place your goals in front of you, nothing but yourself stands in the way of achieving those goals.

Finally, I would like to remind you that your parents/support team are always just a phone call or text away. I am almost certain that if you call your support team, they would love to talk to you and provide you with their love and support.

Although I am not a mental health expert, I have compiled a list of tips that will help you stay positive throughout your college career. I hope these help you stay levelheaded during your college journey. Just remember, if it was easy, everyone would do it.

I. **Have a daily quiet time.** (*The One Year Uncommon Life Daily Challenge* by Tony Dungy is a great choice!) Take time at the beginning or the end of each day to listen, think, and if you're religious, pray. It makes a difference in your day. I cherish my quiet times because it's a break away from the world.

2. **Be patient. It won't last forever.** Whatever you're going through, I promise it won't last long.

3. **Talk to your support team.** Call, text, email! That's what they are for; they want to help you. Find people you can trust with anything.

4. **Stay busy.** This might sound counterintuitive, but staying busy helps keep your mind off things. When I was feeling homesick, it was always at times where I was sitting alone in my room. Get out and try something new!

5. **Take breaks and stay active.** When you get stressed, put down your books, stop worrying, and go do something fun. Go watch a movie, go do something physical you enjoy, or sing a song. These little things will help you in more ways than you realize.

6. **If your anxiety continues, seek professional counselors.** Colleges are filled with folks who are more than willing to talk to you about any issues that you might have. Don't be afraid to get help. It could save your life and turn things around.

PART 2

MAKE THE MOST OF
YOUR ACADEMIC LIFE

"IT'S JUST THE WAY I TALK."

've been told that I talk a little funny, especially when I got to college. I have a bit of what they call a southern twang, and this always became evident when I gave tours of UNC-Chapel Hill. Before I began any tour, I would always preface it with, "Most of you are from out of state, so if you can't understand me, just ask me to repeat myself." Sometimes I would have to repeat myself multiple times, but I still enjoyed sharing my stories with future college students!

Tours on most college campuses are similar. You'll get to see a piece of student life, athletics, dining, housing, and most importantly, academics. I used to tell my tour groups, "Now for the main part of the tour you came to see—the academic section." For some reason, all the parents gave me the nod, and most students rolled their eyes and laughed. But really, academics are the reason that you go to college and will get you where you want to go.

College can be stressful, especially if you're not ready for the coursework, the long nights of studying, and the loads of time that you'll need to devote to school work. I will use this section to help you **Make the Most of Your Academic Life** while in college:

Choosing a Major

You can do it!

Time Management

If you can manage your time wisely in college, you'll figure out the rest with ease.

Exams and Finals Week

This can scare lots of people, but at the end of the day it won't make you, and it won't break you.

Books

Reading is a critical component of your success inside and outside of the classroom.

Study Habits

Learn tips to improve your study habits!

Grades

They're just numbers.

Professors

My favorite part of the academic experience.

Study Abroad

Missing this opportunity is the biggest regret of graduates.

Trust me, no matter how you talk, where you come from, or what major you want to pursue in college, you can **Make the Most** of your academic career.

CHAPTER 8

CHOOSING A MAJOR

"FIND YOUR PASSION."

What's your major? Why do you want to major in that? What are you going to do with that major?" When you get to college, you'll get bombarded with these questions everywhere you go. Choosing a major can be a hard task for some, and although it's a key component for graduation, your major doesn't always affect "what you want to do in life."

Before going to college, I knew that I wanted to be a business major, and I might be one of the rare few that never changed my major or considered changing my major. However, I realize that some students enter college not having any idea what they want their major to be, and I am here to tell you THAT IS COMPLETELY FINE! Sometimes not knowing what you want your major to be can prove to be beneficial. It gives you an opportunity to explore subjects and find your calling.

Wondering how to choose major? Wait no more!

HOW TO CHOOSE YOUR MAJOR

1. **Find your passion.** If you are unsure what you're passionate about, refer back to your goal list. Your goal list can open your eyes to what you really value in this life. Passion can also be found by trying new things, which could include: taking different types of classes, getting involved with different clubs on campus, or anything that gets you out of your dorm room to meet and interact with new people.

2. **Meet with your academic advisor.** Every college campus has an academic advising office. PLEASE TAKE ADVANTAGE OF THIS! Sorry for screaming, but I believe this is one of the most underutilized resources on every college campus. College academic advisors are there to help push you in the right direction with an unbiased point of view. They're also very passionate about helping college students and want to see you succeed.

   Academic advisors can show you potential careers that may fit with each major, and they can also recommend the best class scheduling. Since all schools are different, it's impossible for me to recommend what are the best classes you should take or when you should take them. Reaching out to your advisor will help you answer some of these questions.

3. **Work hard, show up, and participate.** Hard work beats talent—isn't that how the saying goes? That simple statement holds true in college. If you work hard, show up, and participate in your classes, you will reap the benefits. For example, if you choose a major, and never show up for the classes, how will you know if that's the right major?

After choosing a major, it is crucial to plan out what classes you are going to take to get you to graduation. Graduation comes faster than you think, and you want to make sure you are ready on the academic side of things first.

HOW TO ACADEMICALLY GRADUATE IN FOUR YEARS

1. **Take at least fifteen hours per semester, unless you come in with credit.** In order to graduate from most colleges, you need 120 credits/hours, meaning you'll need thirty credits per year or fifteen per semester. Most classes are three credits, and it is very doable to take fifteen credits per semester. Although some students come in with AP, community college, or IB credit, which allows them to take less hours. These high school credits vary from college to college, and I advise checking with the admissions office of your school to see what will transfer as acceptable credit.

2. **Summer School/Overloading/Underloading** Depending on your major, if you want to double major, or your academic workload, you might have to take summer school classes, or overload (taking more than fifteen hours). Summer school classes are just shortened versions of regular classes in the summer time, and can often be easier because you usually only take one or two classes.

On the flip side, during your senior year, you might have the opportunity to "underload." I had the opportunity to take 7.5 hours during my last semester, and let me tell you, it was marvelous. In a later chapter I will talk about my social life, and that wouldn't have been possible without my hard work during the early stages of my college career.

3. **Don't blink.** Four years seems like a long time, but it will truly fly by, and before you know it you will be a senior. Try to enjoy each class you take, no matter how boring they may seem.

Choosing your major can seem like a daunting task. However, I know you will make the right decision if you base it on your passion. I promise you won't be disappointed!

CHAPTER 9

TIME MANAGEMENT

"DON'T COUNT THE HOURS, MAKE THE HOURS COUNT."

My accounting professor, CJ Skender, had a great outlook when it came to managing time. He would always tell us, "Don't count the hours, make the hours count." If you talk to any successful person, they will share that time is their most valuable asset. These people can always make more money and achieve new heights; however, nobody can buy back time (especially successful college students like I know you will become).

Learning to manage your time is one of the most important tools you must acquire to be successful in college. It's important to stress that time management isn't learned in a day, or a week. It's a process that you have to devote yourself to, and although I will share some of my tips and advice for staying on top of your time, it is truly up to you to **Make the Most** of your time.

As I stated before, college can be difficult, especially since there are only twenty-four hours in each day. Time management can be extremely hard because, in my experience, high school didn't prepare me for time management. My schedule was always made for me by the ringing of a bell, my parents were always there to push me along, and I didn't have nearly as much free time. Free time is plentiful in college!

College presented me with many dilemmas during my first semester. "Should I study for this test; should I go out with friends; should I go to the gym; should I go to this club meeting; should I do this or that?" Most colleges have an array of opportunities, which makes college the most unique experience of your life, but those same opportunities can become overwhelming without proper time management.

During my freshman year, my time management skills were tested on a daily basis, especially when it came to writing papers.

When I arrived in my English professor's office I was a bit nervous about what her comments were going to be on my paper. I thought that I had given it effort, but I just had that feeling that she was going to tear it up. I sat down in her small office, prepared to be devastated. She began to explain to me that my detail was exceptional, but I had not followed the prompt. She said that in order to receive a decent grade on the paper I needed to make sure the points followed the prompt clearly.

Since I thought that I put a decent amount of effort into the paper, the only thing that came out was, "Do you think it would be best to start over?" She replied without hesitation, "Yes."

Wait . . . what? NOOOOO! All I could think was I really didn't mean start over. However, I could tell by the look in her eye that starting over was the best possible solution. Then she said, "Times up, any more questions?" I grabbed my book bag and walked out the door and was hit with the pressure of stress and falling raindrops. It was pouring rain that day, and for some reason, I didn't pack an umbrella.

I will be the first to tell you that redoing a five-page paper in one day is not exciting. The walk back to my dorm, after leaving my professor's office, was one of the most important walks I had during my first year. It symbolized everything that college is about. College takes sacrifice. A lot of sacrifice. Sometimes you will be faced with a paper that just has to be rewritten, an exam that will require extra studying, and these things will come at the expense of more fun activities.

It is my hope that you can figure out how to manage your time wisely. If you follow these simple steps, you can drastically change the way you manage your time, and have a step above everyone else!

I. **Make a daily schedule. It's OK to use note cards and sticky notes!** Unlike high school, college professors will outline the entire semester during the first day of class. Very rarely did I have a pop quiz or an assignment that I wasn't told about. Be sure to make a schedule of your exams, papers, and projects. I would advise buying a planner or calendar to record all of these big dates.

    When I would make my schedule, I would always do it the old-school way by writing everything down on a note card. This also helped me keep my head on straight and make sure that I finished what I was supposed to each week. If you are feeling overwhelmed, prioritize your to-dos and complete the most important things first. P.S. I still make schedules like this.

2. **Prioritize. Prioritize. Prioritize. (Check your goals.)** On my first day of college, I dropped the only class I had

that day. I literally walked out of my building, called my dad, and told him I didn't know what to do.

Luckily, I added another class and filled that time window. However, the key thing to understand is that you are no longer going to be in class six to eight hours per day. You might have two classes on Monday, Wednesday, Friday, and maybe three on Tuesday, Thursday. It is critical to prioritize your time and to make sure it is being used wisely.

Don't make me come drag you out of your dorm room!

3. **Breathe and take your time.** College academics can take a lot out of a student. It's OK to walk away from your homework, or to stop studying and take a break. A break can give your brain time to process and understand the material you might not be grasping.

PRACTICE A WORK-DAY MENTALITY

My friend Liddy told me once that her AP English teacher used to tell her class to practice an eight-to-five mentality and treat college like it was their job. Her teacher would tell them to work the eight-hour day as hard as they could, and they would be successful. The teacher told them that some days they'd have to work longer than others. Liddy explained that this mentality helped her be more successful in college and helped hold her accountable.

Time is ticking as you read this chapter. It won't ever stop, and time is not your friend. I was quickly able to realize that college was such a precious time in my life, and in order to accomplish the things I wanted to accomplish, I couldn't waste my time. Ever.

CHAPTER 10

EXAMS AND FINALS WEEK

"STUDY OR STREAK—I'LL LET YOU CHOOSE."

In most colleges the time between fall break and Thanksgiving break is the time for midterm exams. These exams are usually worth a decent portion of your final grade. They can prove to be very difficult and require an immense amount of studying. In my opinion, exams in college are much different than high school exams because of the amount of stress they create and the weight they have toward final grades.

Tests in my high school were given by the plenty and performing badly on one exam/test really didn't set me back or determine my grade in that class. Even though some college classes have a lot of grading opportunities, more often than not, your grade will consist of three or four main exams, so each exam must be taken seriously.

Sometimes exams don't come alone. Some of your classes' exams might fall on the same day, or you might even have all your exams for the entire semester in the same week. Exams can prove to be stressful, but you can't let the stress of college exams dictate your behavior. If you manage your time wisely and release your stress by exercising or doing a fun activity, you will find peace in taking exams.

At the University of North Carolina, there's a tradition that's practiced before every Finals Week. Before sharing this absurd tradition with you, it's probably best to explain Finals Week.

It is a time that sends students into an irregular sleep pattern, creates a tremendous amount of stress, and can be outright brutal to first-year college students. It is a test to see if you can take multiple exams in a small amount of time. Some of it seems irrational, but in order to survive college, you must survive Finals Week.

Now on to the absurd tradition. Each year before Finals Week a large group (way too many, in my opinion) gathers on the top floor of Davis Library (the most popular library on campus) and streaks through the halls, yelling and screaming. Yes, you read that correctly. College students of all shapes, and all sizes, run butt-naked through a library to celebrate Finals Week. I was never a "Finals Streaker" and am still embarrassed to say that I was a viewer (only once). This is just a perfect example of how Finals Week can make people do crazy things to get their minds off studying.

There is a bit of school spirt involved in the naked run through the campus libraries. The streaking ends after the students have made their way into one of the smallest libraries on campus. Once they arrive at their final destination, all of the participants and viewers sing UNC's alma mater.

P.S. There is no need for streaking, but it is still one of the funniest memories of my college experience.

Even though the thought of exams/finals can seem unfathomable, I believe that I found a cure for this stressful time. Trust me, it doesn't involve streaking.

1. **Stay on top of your work.** Getting behind not only hurts your current average and participation grades, but it can set you up for a more stressful exam time. Reading the required materials before each class and turning assignments in on time will help alleviate some of this stress ahead of Finals Week.

2. **Find study partners.** Chances are, if you are struggling, then someone else in your class is struggling. Join up with friends to study; it will make the experience less stressful and more fun.

3. **Make a study plan.** Write down what you are going to study and when you are going to study each day. Do this at least a week in advance and it will allow you time to add to the schedule.

4. **Stay active.** I love to play basketball or run. Don't forget that staying physically active during exams can be beneficial to your exam scores

5. **Sleep**. I know it sounds redundant, but take naps. You will be able to remember much more if you take the time to sleep. I never pulled an all-nighter for an exam and I graduated!

CHAPTER 11

BOOKS

"READ, READ, READ."

Read. Read. Read. I feel like that's something that is continually repeated, no matter what your level of schooling. Unfortunately, I was never a big reader (my SAT score reflected that), but I quickly realized how crucial reading is to your college success.

First things first, if you enjoy reading now, you will have an edge over your other classmates. A lot of the work in college is based on if you did the readings or not. If you did, you are usually prepared for class. Professors will often cold call on students to answer a question from the reading, and nobody wants to be that student who gets called on and hasn't read the material.

If you read your assigned readings ahead of time, you should score significantly better on exams. When I didn't follow this rule, I found my grades weren't as good as they could have been. Read. Read. Read. I will continue to say that because it is so true. I missed multiple questions on exams in my college tenure that I shouldn't have missed because I didn't read the required material.

I completely understand that your Political Science book might be the most boring book that you have ever read, but have some patience—you will reap the benefits on an exam. I will use this chapter to explain two facets of how books are very important to your college career. First, I will discuss books that you will need for your everyday journey. Then I will encourage you to open a book when you have free time and read books that interest you, not just books you have to read for a particular class.

1. **Become a bargain book shopper.** It won't take you long to realize books are MUCH cheaper online than they are in your student book store. Campus bookstores will often mark up their prices because of the convenience factor, but you can wait. Amazon is one of your best friends in college.

   There is one exception to book buying in college and that is how you buy your books during your first semester. At UNC-Chapel Hill, there is a program that allows first-semester, first-year students to preorder their books before they move in. I highly recommend using a service like this (even if it does cost a little extra). This will allow you to have a stress-free book-buying experience. Nobody wants to buy the wrong books before the first day of college. Spend the extra dollars the first semester with the book store, but after you learn the ropes, please venture online.

2. **Read books you enjoy. They will help you relax.** As I stated before, I wasn't a big reader before college, but I have slowly learned to enjoy reading books that interest me. For instance, *Love Does* by Bob Goff was

one of the best books I have ever read, and I read it during some down time during my college career. It tells the story of the author's life that was transformed by love. I have never teared up so much from a book; Goff's stories were truly impactful. Reading books you have interest in can open your eyes to new things, offer an avenue of escape, and allow you to reflect.

You will quickly discover that it is hard to find an extra minute in college to do anything, let alone read books that have nothing to do with class material. I would encourage you to find time to read anyway, whether it be a daily devotional, a sci-fi novel, or an autobiography on someone in the field you want to be in. Find a book and read!

By the way, thanks for picking up my book!

News flash: reading will get you places. It might get you a better grade, it might introduce you to a new passion, and it might prompt you to write a book, like it did me. Reading is more powerful than I ever imagined, you just have to read, read, and read!

STUDY HABITS

"GO THE EXTRA MILE."

Every aspect of college is different, and everyone deals with those aspects in a unique way. Studying is no different, and studying takes practice, especially studying college material.

I mentioned before that high school doesn't really prepare you for the time management piece of college; however, depending on your high school's academic rigor, you might be more than ready for the collegiate level. My experience was not that way. Not to discount my high school, but it just didn't compare to the challenges that I faced while at UNC-Chapel Hill. The classes were more difficult, I had to give each assignment more effort, and there was little room for error. Although I wasn't as prepared as I could have been, my work ethic shined, and I was able to graduate with honor from the Kenan-Flagler Business School. Another example that proves it doesn't matter where you come from, or what high school you went to, you can **Make the Most** of your academic career while in college.

There are so many stories I could share about how my study habits failed, how they succeeded, and even times that I forgot to study, but nothing opened my eyes more than my first exam.

The week before my first exam, my professor informed the class that in order to be successful on her exams, we must spend fifteen hours studying. All I could remember was "Fifteen hours? You have got to be kidding me." Before college, the only exam I studied longer than fifteen hours for was the SAT. I learned that fifteen hours isn't nearly enough time for bigger exams (Finals Week).

I am forever grateful for my first exam because it prepared me for other exams that were much more rigorous. The professor's advice of allotting a certain amount of time for studying helped me get on the right track from the get-go. It's also nice to note that my first exam ever in college was one of the highest exam grades I ever received. (Don't get lazy like me. A good starting point is fifteen hours.)

Below you'll find some of my tips for studying effectively, but as I mentioned, we all study differently. You'll figure it out, just make sure you figure it out quickly.

1. **Study early.** Don't procrastinate. I am sure you have heard this at least a thousand times, but it's so true in college, especially when it comes to studying. You'll find that exams will creep up on you. Be sure to be on top of your schedule so you don't forget upcoming exams. I would advise you to start studying two weeks before your exams come around, which will give you sufficient time to clarify anything that you might not have understood.

2. **Seek tutors, homework help, and office hours.** Don't be afraid to ask someone for help if you are struggling in a subject or class. I pretty much lived in

homework help sessions when I took economics classes. Sometimes material just doesn't click, and in order to be successful in the classroom, you have to go the extra mile. Remember when I said that my work ethic made me successful? Long nights in homework sessions will get you places!

Don't stress if material in a certain class isn't clicking for you and doesn't make sense. Sometimes, you will take classes in college that require you to work ten times harder than other people in your class to receive the same grade. Just remember that we all have our different strengths, and if yours isn't biology, don't sweat it, just work hard to make the required grade.

Most professors are required to have office hours. Office hours are allotted times that professors are at your disposal, and most times these take place in their office. This is a great opportunity to get help on a topic you don't understand, and to also get to know the professor. You never know what going to office hours can do for you. For example, what if you're on the borderline of making an A-, but you have an 89.4? A professor that knows you is more likely to give you the bump that gives you an A-.

3. **Make study guides.** Make real study guides. Not the study guides that might be on a Google Doc (a resource that you will use frequently to collaborate with other students), or ones where you copy and paste notes onto a Word document. Actually write notes about the material that will be covered on a piece of paper. This is more time consuming, but it is a proven fact that if you write things down, you are more likely to remember them. After I wrote my study guides out, I would carry them with me

everywhere and read them any time I had a spare moment. Studying truly does pay off, but I will be the first to tell you that it is what you make of it. If you dread studying, and put it off until the last minute, you will not reap the benefits. Now, I understand there are some geniuses out there, but I wasn't one of those folks. Work hard, put in the effort, go the extra mile, and you will see results.

Think about it this way: the more you study and harder you work, the more that you will get to enjoy the fruits of your labor at another time.

CHAPTER 13

GRADES

"DO YOUR BEST AND YOU'LL HAVE NOTHING TO WORRY ABOUT."

With all of this talk about exams, studying, and books, it's appropriate to talk about the thing that can either make or break your day—grades. Grades in college might be different than you are accustomed to (all depending on your high school or precollege academia). They were different to me in a few ways: they were on a different grade scale, they weren't as nice to me (my grades were much better in high school), but I learned to accept them.

On the first day of class at UNC-Chapel Hill, one of the oldest traditions is to drink from the Old Well. The Old Well is one of the most iconic landmarks on campus and legend has it, "if you drink from the Old Well on the first day of class, you will get a 4.0 that semester." That legend was just a legend for my college journey, as I never received a 4.0 in a semester. Here a few things to know about making grades:

1. **It's highly likely that you're not going to be the smartest person in the class.** In high school I was your typical teacher's pet. I always turned my assignments in on time, I made good grades, and I would come prepared for class. I graduated in the top 10 percent of my graduating class and figured that I could continue my same academic success in college. High school didn't pose much of a challenge for me, at least not like college did.

   When I arrived at orientation, the admissions team started rattling off statistics about the students sitting around me. I learned there were so many talented, smart, and ambitious students in my class. College is filled with thousands of students who were the top of their class in high school, some might have even been valedictorian of their school. After leaving orientation, I realized that if there were all of these academically talented students around me, grading and assignments were going to be that much harder.

   Quick lesson: this isn't meant to scare you, but should excite you. During a trip to California I was told by an early Google investor, "If you're ever the smartest person in the room, get out!"

2. **Set goals for what kind of grades you want to make.** Set your goals for grades based on the type of student you want to be. If you need a certain GPA to get into grad school, make that your goal. If you want to make the Dean's List (3.5 or higher, usually an A/B average), make that your goal. It was my goal to make the Dean's List four of the eight semesters I was in college. I was able to make that dream a reality during my last semester.

3. **Grades can be curved.** You will get grades back that make you want to vomit. Well, maybe not if you

are brilliant, but in my experience, everyone fails an exam. However, most professors won't let one exam grade affect your total outcome in the course if you have put forth effort. Professors will sometimes curve exams and grades at the end of the semester. For example, if you made a sixty-five on an exam, that might be a seventy-five once they curve it. Just be patient and work hard on other assignments.

Remember when I mentioned "work ethic?" This is where it comes into play. Attending those homework/tutoring sessions also helps boost grades.

4. **Learn to accept grades.** Don't let grades define your college career. They are just a number, and in a few months, you will forget about them. When I learned to accept grades, and to move on, I found the classroom to be a happier place. No story tells how I adjusted to grades in college better than my experience with my Italian class.

    At UNC-Chapel Hill, one of the academic requirements for each student is to have at least three levels of a foreign language. I chose to take Italian. Before college I had no experience with the language; I just thought it would be interesting. On the first day of class I was greeted by the professor, who immediately started speaking to me in Italian. I quickly froze because I didn't know how to respond. I still remember that class like it was yesterday, not because I didn't understand anything the professor was saying, but because of the phone call I had with my mom after the class.

    I called my mom, mainly to get her permission to drop the class and ask her what other language I should take. My plans quickly changed as my mother told me to "suck it up." My mom explained to me that college is supposed to challenge you. Sometimes you won't understand material and you have to be patient. That simple, honest conversation encouraged me to press on. Although the journey was long, I survived all three language classes. I even high-fived my last Italian professor on my way out the door.

I learned quickly in my college career that sometimes you won't make the grades you want. In some cases, classes or topics will literally sound foreign to you. Learning to accept the grades you make will give you all the peace you'll need in the classroom. Just do your best, and you won't have anything to worry about.

CHAPTER 14

PROFESSORS

"INTRODUCE YOURSELF."

He's six feet tall, white-headed, mid-sixties, and he began working in the business field before the students in his audience were even a thought. His energy is contagious as he runs around the classroom demanding input from the fifteen students. He has more spunk than any of the other students in the class, despite only being an adjunct professor (he's paid much less than a regular professor). The class, Consulting for the Entrepreneurial Firm, is held once a week from five to seven thirty. As you might notice, the class is held right in the middle of dinner time, which for college students is a big deal. However, the professor's passion to teach business is very fulfilling, allowing students to postpone their dinner plans.

Professors are incredible. They are not scary or mean; they are people who are super passionate about helping students learn. The story above is a true story. These experiences with my professors weren't odd occurrences. I rarely had an experience where I didn't enjoy the professor teaching my class. All professors are different and offer a different element of teaching and material, but most are genuine and will do anything to help you!

Before coming to college, I had this stereotype built up in my head that professors were just these really smart people that spoke to huge classes, and that's all they did. I never thought it would be possible to get to know them, to go to lunch with them, and to build such a strong relationship that I would want to invite a former professor of mine to my wedding.

Now, you might be wondering, why in the world would you want to build a relationship with a professor? The answer is really simple. Reaching out to your professors is a must-do in college. The theme of this book is to **Make the Most** of your college experience, and you can't do that unless you **Make the Most** of your professors. They aren't just people teaching a subject, they are passionate educators who want to enrich the lives of the students that take their class.

Here are some tips on how to reach out to professors, what to talk about, and ways they can help:

1. **Introduce yourself on the first day of class.** This is a simple one, but crucial. On the first day of class (either before or after), make sure you introduce yourself to all of your professors – no matter if the class has ten students in it or five hundred. Shake their hand, look them in the eye, and let them know that you are excited to take their course (even if you aren't).

2. **Email them to schedule a lunch date.** I have never met a stranger, and I will talk to anyone, but for some reason eating lunch with my professors used to make me nervous. Don't feel nervous. Reach out to your professor via email and ask them to lunch or coffee. I would wait a few weeks into the semester before

asking them, but I think it's important that you build relationships with some of your professors. Please note, I am not telling you to go to lunch with every single one of your professors, but one, maybe two per semester.

My university had a program called "Meals with Heels" that linked professors/students for lunch dates. The university would actually pay for both of you to go eat somewhere on campus. I took full advantage of the program and would even joke with my tour guide groups, "Out of my four 'Meals with Heels' experiences, I received three out of four A's in those classes." You truly never know if meeting with a professor can get you a better grade, or even land you a job!

3. **Keep in touch.** It is important to maintain relationships with your professors following the semester you take their class. If you truly found a connection with the professor, make sure you continue meeting with them, and using them as a resource.

I can share countless stories of how professors impacted my college career. Professors gave me someone to share my passions with, someone to pitch business ideas to, and befriend. I found that most of my professors were more than willing to sit down with me, and through that process, I was able to build a small network of professors that I can call on at any time. They truly are special people, no matter their age, spunk, or the subject they teach. Never be scared to reach out!

CHAPTER 15

STUDY ABROAD

"GO SEE FOR YOURSELF"

Out of all of the successful college students I know, if they have any regrets, it's usually one thing—they didn't study abroad. "I wish I would have just made the sacrifice and gone somewhere!" they tell me. But, hey, you're not going to be one of those people, you are going to study abroad in some way, shape, or fashion.

Studying abroad is a remarkable experience. Most universities have study abroad programs in about every country imaginable, and if they don't, they have a brother/sister university that does. Programs vary in length – there are year-long, semester, summer, and even two-week programs.

Don't make excuses for not studying abroad. Here are some of the top excuses that I have heard and the reasons why they don't make any sense:

1. **"I don't have time."**
   Listen here. There's time if you make time, and a study-abroad experience is one of the most unique

learning opportunities out there. It's well worth your
time and energy to study abroad, especially with the
flexibility of programs!

2. **"I don't have the money."**
   Again, neither did I! Money shouldn't be a determi-
   nant when studying abroad. I received a scholarship
   and took a small loan, and it was by far the most well
   spent money of my college career.

3. **"I'm scared I'll miss out."**
   Some students think they will miss out on a big
   sporting event or social life with their friends. Again,
   you are only missing out if you don't study abroad.
   Your friends will be jealous of you because you took
   the leap of faith to study in a foreign country.

Like most students do in college, I procrastinated. I procrastinated my trip abroad because I was a little scared about
going, but during my junior summer I boarded a plane to
South Africa for a two-week program.

My program consisted of visiting Johannesburg and
Cape Town, each city for about one week. I was joined by
thirty-one of my fellow business students, and three faculty
advisors. Traveling to South Africa was a huge step out of
my comfort zone, 8,027 miles out of my comfort zone to be
exact. In total, the flights took twenty-plus hours, consisting
of a layover in London and a twelve-hour flight across the
continent of Africa.

JOHANNESBURG (JO'BURG)

Before making the trek to South Africa, I had very clouded
views of the country. The American media had polluted
my mind with sights of animals running wild, dry deserted
towns, and no hope for opportunity. However, I quickly
learned all of that was false.

During our first day we visited the African Leadership Academy (ALA). The ALA is an academy similar to a high school, but the students are between the ages of sixteen to nineteen and come from forty-four African countries. The school has a lower acceptance rate than Harvard. While at the ALA, we spoke with a few of their bright students about some of their entrepreneurial endeavors. One of them, Genesis, a young guy from Cameroon, was interested in starting his own paper bag company that would help with the high unemployment rates of his home country. Hearing the stories from these students was such an eye-opening experience for my career. Each student was more passionate about helping their community than making a profit.

While in Johannesburg we stayed in an affluent area, so affluent that we were in the richest square mile of all of Africa. Wealth in South Africa is not distributed equally. There's a 50 percent unemployment rate and the average person lives on $1.50 a day. Just outside of the little affluent area I was staying were seven hundred thousand South Africans that live in strict poverty. Seeing this disparity, our group's perspective changed, and we realized how fortunate we were to live in the United States.

During our trip we ventured to Soweto, the home of Nelson Mandela. On the drive from Jo'burg to Soweto, we slowly saw a change in scenery. The large houses with even bigger fences began to disappear, and the small shacks began to multiply. While in the township, we saw a protest in which the citizens of Soweto were protesting the load shedding issue in South Africa. In order to conserve energy for the country, the government has to shut down power for extended periods of time, which is slowing the growth of their economy.

We also got to visit a local restaurant called Sakhumzi. The food was very different. They served intestines, lamb, and some other things that I can't even describe. I can't say that I would ever venture back to the restaurant in Soweto, but again, this was part of the experience, and something that made the trip that much more memorable.

My favorite part about Jo'burg was meeting local entrepreneurs and hearing their life stories. One individual, Askar, was a Somalian that ventured to South Africa while he was a young teenager. He made his way by boat, car, bus, and train, until he eventually arrived with only the clothes on his back. However, he didn't let his lack of resources hold him back. He became a hawker, someone that sells arts and crafts to tourists. This job was very dangerous because he had to travel from Jo'burg to Cape Town by train with all of his goods. On one occasion, he came face to face with a thief, who stabbed him in the stomach with a knife. Luckily, he made it to the hospital in time for a quick recovery.

As Askar told his story, I was inspired. Not just because he defied the odds, but because he never gave up. He was one of the sincerest individuals I have ever met. He continued to tell us that he started a local supermarket after he quit selling goods on the street, which eventually got him to where he is today, working for one of the largest banks in the World.

CAPE TOWN

After about a week in Jo'burg, we hopped on a two-hour plane ride to Cape Town. Most of the group was more excited about Cape Town because it is known for being a more touristy area and has been compared geographically to San Francisco. With my first glimpse of Cape Town from the airplane, I, too, could see the resemblance.

Our week in Cape Town was a lot like our week in Jo'burg, but with a few added bonuses. We heard from many different speakers, saw different companies, and visited townships, but we also got to go on a safari and swim with great white sharks.

In our time at Mflueni, a small township in Cape Town, we interacted with the entrepreneurs yet again. This time, however, we were selling SIM cards and winter coats on the street. This was another huge learning experience because selling items to people who live in poverty is an extremely difficult task. In the end, our group only sold one SIM card.

As you might have guessed, some of the academic parts of the trip weren't as exciting as selling SIM cards to local South Africans. However, experiencing the events with thirty-one classmates made the academic sessions worthwhile.

Following the final session, we had dinner and went straight to bed because at 5:15 a.m., twenty-five of us boarded a bus to swim with great white sharks. Yeah, you heard me, great whites.

In case you didn't know, South Africa is home to "shark alley." Every year Discovery Channel films great white sharks at "shark alley" for their features on *Shark Week*. When Discovery Channel isn't there filming, they let tourists like myself and my classmates get into a cage surrounded by water, right where those big sharks swim.

As the boat made its way from the shore, I began to get more and more nervous. Then the eight-person cage was dropped into the water, and the "chum man" started chumming. Within minutes, a large gray object darted by, probably nine feet long, a "small one," the guides said.

Being the impatient one, I wanted to be one of the first in the water. I nervously pulled on the wet suit, strapped on a GoPro camera, and hopped into the water.

"Left, down, down, down," the guide yelled as great whites darted by the cage. I remember coming up out of the water yelling in excitement. This was the coolest thing I had ever done. During some parts of the dive, I thought

I was watching a video, it seemed so unreal. Then, all of a sudden, this huge object appeared from my right side. "Was that Megalodon?" I screamed at the guide.

Megalodon was this huge dinosaur-like shark that the people from Discovery Channel made an entire show about one year during *Shark Week*. He laughed and said no, but it was one of the biggest sharks they had seen in years. It was roughly five meters, which is over sixteen feet long.

I could go on and on about my experience abroad, but it wouldn't do it justice. You have to go have the experiences for yourself. No matter the cost, a trip in another country with students and friends your age is priceless.

When I applied to go to South Africa, I really didn't know why I wanted to go. Yes, it was a goal of mine to study abroad for some time, but I didn't know why exactly. The trip abroad allowed me to meet new people, learn new, exciting things, and be humbled. The people in the townships lived in houses that most people in America wouldn't consider a house. However, these people love their community, they are not giving up, and they are super optimistic about the future.

GO, JUST GO

- Visit your school's study abroad office.
- Find the right program that fits your schedule. I couldn't do a semester-long program because I would've missed my mama's cooking. Do what fits you best!
- Fund your program through scholarships and loans if you have to.
- Choose the location that most excites you. South Africa excited me because it was so far away. It was

way different than other programs, and it gave me the opportunity to meet a real life Jaws.

During one of the last nights of my study-abroad trip, one of the guys on the trip reminded me of an old analogy. "There are two clocks in this world: a world clock, which is circular, and your clock, which is an hour glass."

Time is not on your side, so you must do **great big things** while here on Earth. Maybe it's singing your school's alma mater in a foreign country or making small talk with a stranger on a plane. Just go! Time is wasting.

PART 3

MAKE THE MOST OF YOUR SOCIAL LIFE

"LIVE FOR THE MOMENT."

It only takes a few seconds for the Dean E. Smith Center (UNC's basketball arena) to become a nightmare for the opposing team. Fans from all levels of the stadium, row A to row ZZ, stand and create an electric atmosphere like no other. During my time as a Tar Heel student and lifelong fan, I experienced what it means to bleed Carolina blue in about every way possible. I've been in the upper deck, lower deck, in the student section dressed as a banana, and on the court as a JV basketball manager.

School spirit was just a piece of my social life as a college student, but my school spirt brought most of my social aspects together. Spending time with friends, cheering on our team, and going crazy after big games are some of my fondest memories when I look back on my college experience. It doesn't matter where you go to school or what colors you represent, make sure that you fully entrench yourself in the culture.

No memory more encompasses my social life than the UNC-Duke basketball game during my sophomore year. If you're not familiar with the UNC-Duke basketball rivalry, let me educate you.

Since 1920, the UNC-Duke game has been one of the most anticipated match-ups of the season. The rivalry schools, which are only separated by eight miles, have created some of the most memorable basketball games in the history of the sport. The two schools have produced numerous hall of famers, countless championships for their fans, and dozens of unforgettable finishes. Most basketball fans put the UNC-Duke game on their sports bucket list.

When I came to Carolina, I was well aware of the rivalry and had grown up watching the Heels beat the Blue Devils on many occasions. However, all of the victories I had experienced were through television or radio. During my first three years at UNC-CH, we had not beaten Duke in football or basketball. I was beginning to think that I had brought some sort of bad luck to the program. My UNC-Duke record as a student before February 20, 2014 was 0-4; we had two losses in football and two in basketball.

During my sophomore and junior years, I was a JV basketball manager for the team, and this allowed me to have some of the best seats in the arena. I was especially grateful for these seats during my sophomore year because it was the only year that UNC beat Duke at home while I was a student.

The game lived up to all of my expectations. The crowd was rockin' the entire game. The only times that the 21,750 fans sat down were during timeouts and halftime. Later, my parents told me that when they were watching the game on TV, it felt as if the screen was shaking.

We were losing almost the entire game, but every time Duke made a run, we had a run of our own. It reminded me of a tennis match; Coach Roy Williams would make a decision and then there would be a countermove by Coach Mike Krzyzewski. Even though I missed a few minutes of the second half due to my manager duties, I caught the last few crucial minutes of the game. These crucial minutes were fueled by a raging comeback, which eventually gave us the lead.

It wouldn't make sense for me to give you the play-by-play of the last two minutes, but I think you can figure out how the game turned out. Instead of recapping the last minutes, I want to emphasize the meaning of "living in the moment."

As the clock hit zero and my Heels secured the victory, something special happened. In a matter of seconds, the Dean Dome floor was filled with fans of all ages, screaming, jumping, and fist-pumping. And then I joined them. I took off my "manager tag" and happily put on my "student tag," because this moment was special. Carolina had won the game 74–66.

Rushing the court after a win against your arch rival is a surreal experience. I was chest bumping with people I had never met, screaming until I couldn't scream anymore, and feeling as if I was in a dream. For a few brief minutes, I gave life everything I had; I was living in the moment.

I have found that it's not often that we as humans get to experience situations like the one I witnessed. Our lives are too predictable. We go to grade school for twelve years, some of us go to college, and most of us will have families, get a job . . . and so on. This cycle has become a part of our culture. However, what if we lived for "the moment" every day? What if people (including myself) woke up every morning with an upbeat and positive attitude to storm the court called life? The answer is simple. We would become better people and we would experience life in a different, much more enjoyable way.

My experience of rushing the court with some of my closest friends was one of the coolest experiences I had during my time in college. Cheering for your school and channeling your school spirit is just one way that your social life can flourish during college.

In the coming chapters, I will explain several areas of your college experience that can impact your social life during school:

Roommates and Housing
Don't be scared of random roommates.

Relationships and Hookups
What your parents won't share with you, I will.

Party Scene
It's all about how and when you choose to party.

Intramurals and Clubs
We all have our place outside the classroom.

Sporting Events
"Hey mom! I'm on TV!"

Greek Life
Determine if a fraternity or sorority is right for you.

I received some of the best precollege advice from my cousin, Jason, who had just graduated. "Austin, college is all about choices. You can make good choices or bad choices. It's your choice." That's all he had to say to get me on the right track socially before entering college.

CHAPTER 16

ROOMMATES AND HOUSING

"LET'S HAVE PASTA PARTIES."

One of the biggest decisions you'll make before getting to college is who you are going to live with. At most universities, first-year students are required to live on campus, and this usually requires you to live with a roommate. This roommate can be a friend from your high school, or you can take a step out of your comfort zone, and go for the random roommate track.

I highly recommend taking a leap of faith and rooming with someone completely random. College is about making new friends, and if you have a best friend going to the same college as you, they will still be your friend if you don't live with them. But if you don't give someone else a chance, someone random, you never know who you will miss out on getting to meet.

During my time in college, I lived on campus for three years and enjoyed every second of it. Sometimes it was hard, sometimes I didn't get along with my roommates, and sometimes it seemed unbearable. However, looking back on my college career, I wouldn't have changed it for the world because there's something about sharing a ten by fifteen room with someone you don't know that makes you grow up.

It's important to note that I lived in all kinds of housing options during my time in college. I lived in a traditional-style dorm (hall style with a shared bathroom among twenty-plus students), a suite-style dorm (shared bathroom with five other guys), and I ended my college career in an old dilapidated house that holds some of my best memories (Church Street Pasta Parties).

Out of respect for my former roommates, I won't share any negative stories in regards to any of my ex-roomies. However, you do need to realize that there will be instances of drama and times where you and your roommate will need to talk things out to work through any conflicts that might arise. For example, you might have different sleeping patterns, or you might want to have friends over that they might not like. You will be different from your roommate.

LIVING WITH A ROOMMATE

- Go random, it's well worth the experience!
- Respect your roommate's belongings. No matter what kind of dorm, apartment, or house you live in, always respect someone else's things.
- If you're going to stay up late, make sure that you are not affecting your roommates' sleeping patterns.
- Everyone has opinions; respect your roommates'. Nobody wants to live with someone they can't stand.
- Get to know them, visit their hometown, or go on trips together. Do whatever it takes to see them for the person they are.

There were instances in my four years where I didn't have the best living experiences. However, I can count those times on one hand. I truly **Made the Most** of my living experiences by living with different people. College allowed me the opportunity to live with some of the best people this world has to offer and to make unforgettable memories.

Living on Church Street in Chapel Hill was by far something that I will never forget, and it was all because of pasta.

It took some convincing, but my parents allowed me to live off campus my senior year. I used some of my negotiating tactics I had learned in class, and after a few weeks, they agreed.

Living off campus can vary from college to college. Depending on where you go to college, you might live on campus all four years, or you might only live on campus one year. It truly depends on the norms of the university and what is required. I enjoyed living on campus because it allowed me to be in the center of the action. However, during my senior year, I wanted a bit more freedom.

During my sophomore year, my friend Mitch pitched this simple idea to us that wouldn't come to fruition until our senior year. "Let's all get a house (at the time he was speaking to my four other roommates and myself) senior year and have pasta parties." We looked at him like he was crazy. "You know, like cook a bunch of pasta, have a bunch of people over, it will be awesome." To be honest, at that point in time, I never thought my parents would allow me to live off campus, so I didn't pay much attention to him.

After signing the lease to rent the house for our senior year, I remember seeing the excitement in Mitch's eyes. His pasta-party dream would soon come to life.

At first, I think people thought we were joking when we said we were going to have pasta parties. One of my friends asked, "Is pasta code for something else?" I quickly reassured him that we would be eating pasta and hanging out. For a more detailed definition, see below:

Pasta Parties – inviting your friends over for a casual pasta dinner on a Friday night for a time of fellowship, laughs, and a great time.

These pasta parties became a huge hit and were something I looked forward to each month. We recruited two of our friends to do the cooking, and Mitch and I acted as the hosts. Not only did I buy into Mitch's vision, but others loved the concept, too. It was by far the best type of party I attended during my time in college. During the final pasta party, we even had a solo artist perform. Funny enough, this artist was the same person who questioned the actual meaning of pasta before. (Love you, Jon Allis!)

Moving into college housing is exciting; heck, it's exciting every single year that you get to do it. Each year is different, and each year you pack new things. For example, you don't have to pack a bed when you move into a dorm, but it's needed when you move off campus!

Living with different people is also exciting. I truly never knew what it meant to have a super close friend until coming to college. In high school, you probably have one or two best friends who you see at school, and maybe on the weekends. In college, you wake up beside this person and might see them all day long. I will forever cherish my roommates in college and they will be my forever friends.

CHAPTER 17

RELATIONSHIPS AND HOOKUPS

"THE GOOD, THE BAD, AND THE UGLY."

Out of all of the different topics in this book, this chapter took me the longest to write. Relationships in college can be wonderful, and you'll meet some of your lifelong friends. Some will even meet their future spouse. However, relationships in college can be weird, overwhelming, and very confusing. The following chapter is my account of how I was affected by the different relationships in college, and how some were good, bad, and ugly.

When you arrive at college, you will meet so many people that you won't be able to remember the names everyone you met. You will get to meet professors from all walks of life, and hopefully, if you follow my instructions, you will get to know some of them on a more personal level. There are so many different people you will get to meet in college, and it's truly up to you to **Make the Most** of those opportunities that present themselves. When I look back on my college career, the people are what I miss the most.

Before coming to college, I decided to end my relationship with my high school sweetheart because of the distance issue. I thought it would be in my best interest to enter college with a clear mind. This decision didn't come easy because I had dated my girlfriend for more than eighteen months. I'm not telling you to break up with your girlfriend/boyfriend right now if you are going to college without them, but I am telling you to think about it. Think long and hard about what it will take to keep your relationship afloat. If you are willing to put in the work to maintain trust, you might consider staying together.

I came to college thinking it was all going to be easy. I would walk into my freshman year, find the woman of my dreams, and one day marry her. That, my friends, is a rare example, and in my situation, it didn't exactly work out that way.

In my early college years, I was super focused on my school work and extracurricular activities. Even though the girl to guy ratio at UNC was 60:40, I kept my mind focused and didn't pursue any relationships with women. Now, this doesn't mean that I didn't go on dates. I was very friendly, but I didn't pursue women like I did during the end of my college career.

Although the journey of my college career had glorious relationships, there was a moment that sent me into a time of confusion. At the beginning of my senior year, I entered a phase of my college journey that I called my "wild streak."

It's important to note that before coming to college, it was my goal to "be a virgin until I get married." That goal comes from a variety of reasons: my religious background, my willingness to respect my future wife, and because I knew that having sex would get me into more trouble than it would help me. I am proud to say that I kept that promise to myself and am still a virgin. However, there were lots of times that my goal to do so was challenged, especially when I was under the influence of alcohol.

During my senior year I had less hours in the classroom, a job offer, and more time to do fun things that revolved around my social life. I was also twenty-one years old, so that gave me full freedom. I could go into any bar or club I wanted, and I could buy alcohol. In the following chapter, I will talk more about drinking, but for now, I will just tell you that the freedom felt great – you truly feel like you can do whatever you want.

With twelve hours my first semester and seven hours my second semester (I was able to underload because of my previous overloading semesters), I had set myself up for a senior year filled with "doing whatever I wanted to do."

My "wild streak" only lasted a few months, and it consisted of me getting drunk too many times to count. My roommate and I even called one week a "marathon week" because we went out to bars every night for a week straight. We were totally exhausted by the end of the week, and in hindsight, it was truly silly and did nothing to benefit me. This "wild streak" also consisted of me hooking up with random girls, which left me confused.

I can recall when my "streak" ended because I remember sitting in my car, calling my mom, and telling her about my struggles. Do you remember when I told you to build a support team? Well, here is a prime example of when a key member of my support team, my mama, came in extra handy.

After a long conversation with my mom, I concluded that the previous months of my life weren't a true depiction of the person I was. I wasn't a drunk, I wasn't a player, and I wasn't a person who disrespected others. My "wild streak" wasn't me, and in the moment I couldn't see that.

I could just see the short-term happiness that getting drunk and fooling around was bringing me.

It would be unfair for me to tell you that getting drunk and hooking up wasn't fun in the moment. However, those acts provided only short-term happiness. When you wake up and regret the thing you did the night before, or with a huge headache (hangover), then you know you made the wrong decision. After I realized that alcohol, hookups, and doing whatever I wanted was only going to give me this short-term feeling, I got out. I wanted something much more—I wanted long-term happiness. Long-term happiness isn't found behind a bottle or in a bedroom. It's found in yourself, and you have to learn that on your own time. However, I wouldn't trade my experience because it taught me so much about myself.

I share this with all of you because I want you to know that relationships are a beautiful thing. They can also be catastrophic to your college career. Luckily for me, I was never in any terrible relationships in college, but this is a warning to you to be careful. Sleeping around will get you nowhere in college; seriously, it's all short-term happiness.

Now to a more serious topic.

Sexual assault and alcohol on college campuses are a scary, scary combo. Many cases of reported rape have included the victim and/or the accused being drunk or under the influence. If you choose to be intimate with someone, make sure both of you have the ability to consent.

For a better understanding of this topic, check out the "Tea Consent" video on YouTube.

College is a unique place, and with that comes unique and great relationships. I met some of my lifelong friends in college, and those are the ones you always hear about. You hear about the parents who met in college and fell in love, or the first-year roommates who became best friends and were in each other's weddings, but it doesn't always happen that way. College is meant for you to **Make the Most** of your relationships, the good, bad, and the ugly. So, don't waste a second being silly or chasing short-term happiness.

Below are some of my thoughts, ideas, and advice on how to **Make the Most** of your relationships.

1. **Stay true to who you are**. I know that sounds cliché, and weird, but do it.

2. **Listen to your friends, but really listen to yourself.** If you deep down have feelings for someone that aren't just physical feelings, don't run from them—hold on tight.

3. **Be honest**. Never lie about your feelings. Honesty hurts. Man, does it hurt. However, honesty is the best way to let someone know how you feel, and I believe in letting feelings flow. Don't hold them back.

4. **Hookups happen.** I didn't think they did, but they do. They happen a lot in college, but remember that's only short-term happiness.

5. **Don't be afraid.** Don't be scared to meet new people. It's OK to kiss a lot of people; just make sure you're not passing around the mono virus.

6. **You're still young.** Don't get fixated on one person. Play the field, but do it respectfully. Don't mess around with multiple people at the same time. That can prove to be reckless.

7. **Apologize.** It's never too late to ask someone for forgiveness.

8. **Learn fast.** Try and learn as much as you can about what you want from your significant other before finding them. Then don't let go.

9. **Pray**. Something I neglected during my wild streak. I believe that God really knows the way, and everything that you experience is for some greater plan.

10. **Respect others.** Relationships are a two-way street. Treat the other person with complete respect.

CHAPTER 18

PARTY SCENE

"GET DRUNK ON LIFE!"

College has the stereotype of being a place to party and let loose. A song called "I Love College" by Asher Roth was popular during my high school days, and it helped build that stereotype. The song gives this picture of college that is all about drinking and partying, and that scared me.

Before arriving to college, I had never had a sip of alcohol, and at the beginning of my college career, it was my goal to wait until I was legal to try it.

Looking back, it's very interesting to see how my behavior changed from freshman to senior year. I went from being a person who literally looked down on drinking to someone who went buck-wild crazy his senior year. By being on opposite ends of the spectrum, I was able to assess both sides of the story. I'll use this chapter to give you my two tales and what I think is the best route to take.

During high school, I was dead set on waiting until I was legal to have my first sip of alcohol. I would stay away from the parties that had alcohol, and was even reluctant to go out because I was afraid of being pressured to drink. I could always avoid the pressures if I wanted to. I could go home, or fall back on my parents if I didn't want to go to a party. "My parents won't let me come to your party, sorry!" I would tell my friends.

However, this all changed in college. The temptations of drinking were right in my face during my first year, and the thought of drinking underage scared me to no end.

I can remember my first fraternity party like it was yesterday. It was a Halloween party, and it was in a really shady-looking garage. The music was super loud, the garage was steaming, and the air reeked of cheap beer and marijuana. Until you experience it, you won't know, but this is a typical college party. The party made me uncomfortable in so many ways, and it didn't help that people kept offering me drinks. Luckily, the folks I was with didn't want to stay long either, so we dipped out early and headed to get some late-night food.

Looking back on that night, it doesn't seem like a big deal to me anymore. However, at the time I was a small-town kid who hadn't seen much. I had never been right in the middle of a party that made me feel that uncomfortable and had never been in a place that I wanted to leave as soon as I arrived. However, my entire college career didn't only consist of me being uncomfortable at parties. Oh no, I became very comfortable, so comfortable that I forgot who I truly was.

It's a task to truly **Make the Most** of your college experience. In order to do so, you have to keep your head on straight, work hard, and learn to focus when the time comes.

During my time in college, I focused on three areas: my academics, my opportunities, and my social life. What's unique about this is that I gave each area my attention at different times. My first two years were primarily focused on my academics (getting accepted into the business school), my third year was focused on my opportunities (coming in a later chapter), and finally, my senior year was focused on my social life. I didn't plan it to happen that way, but I knew in order to be successful in college I had to have my academics in line. It would have been nearly impossible to have been focused on my social life and academics at the same time, with the same amount of effort I gave both.

I mentioned earlier, my goal was to wait until I was legal before drinking any alcohol. Technically, I achieved that goal. I was nineteen and I was in London, where the legal drinking age is eighteen.

My first sip of alcohol came at the tallest building in Europe called The Shard. Since I was legal, and since this was the first time I had ever traveled out of the country, I knew this would be a perfect time to try an alcoholic beverage. However, if you decide to let your buddy's dad order you a drink, make sure it's for a first-timer. I ended up going with his regular choice: a Jack Daniels and Diet Coke, which isn't the best choice for a first drink.

I had imagined that moment being some breathtaking event where I would instantly get drunk. As you can imagine, I didn't get drunk, and I realized that Jack and Diet Coke would never be my drink of choice.

Following my first sip of alcohol, nothing really wild transpired. I went back to the United States and lived the same life I had lived before, not drinking and honestly having the time of my life. However, during my junior year, I had a few more sips and experienced my first buzz. A buzz is different for every person, but it's when you can feel alcohol kicking in. Nothing much more happened my junior year, and things didn't start getting wild for me until my twenty-first birthday.

In my opinion, your twenty-first birthday is the most fun. It's a time where you officially become a real adult, and there's really nothing else you can't do in this world. For me, and for a lot of other college students that turned twenty-one during their college career, it was a time to get super-duper drunk. I do have to admit, I never thought I would get as drunk as I did that night, but when you don't drink responsibly you end up drinking more than you can remember. In the moment you don't realize how much alcohol you are consuming. You don't fully realize it until you're throwing is all back up. Wait a minute, was that night really fun? Yeah, it was fun to get to hang out with my friends, but what was fun about drinking a substance that didn't taste good and eventually made me puke my guts out? (excuse the graphic imagery)

I wish I could tell you that I learned my lesson after my twenty-first birthday, but I didn't. I continued my wild ride throughout my senior year, got sick, and regretted the things I did. Alcohol and going out to bars became a regular thing for me, and most of my friends weren't used to seeing me that way. "Austin is drunk. I've never seen him like that," one of our friends whispered in my roommate's ear during a night out on the town. You'd think after a concerned comment like that, I would've gotten the memo, but no, I didn't.

My wild streak of going out, getting drunk, and making bad decisions finally came to an end during the spring of my senior year. The streak taught me a lot about myself and about my college career. I learned that wasn't the person I wanted to be and I didn't want alcohol to become a staple in my life, like it was during my senior year. I also learned that partying and school deadlines don't really work together. You can either be successful in your school work, or you can party hard. Some can find an in-between, but thank goodness I was only rowdy after I had most of my schooling complete.

With my experiences comes a few pieces of advice, and these tips should help you choose the way that will help you **Make the Most** of the party scene in college. I know that sounds weird, but I always joked and said "I'm drunk on life! Why do I need alcohol?"

1. **If you drink, drink responsibly and drink legally.** I understand most won't listen to me, but I truly think this will help you out tremendously. Wait to party later!

2. **Shots will catch up to you.** Alcohol shots aren't the only ones that catch up to you. Other parts of your life can be affected by partying too much.

3. **Focus.** If you are going to focus on **Making the Most** of your academic career, do that. It's nearly impossible to focus on partying and school at the same time.

4. **You can still party sober.** You can still party and not drink. Heck, you can be the life of the party and never take a sip of alcohol.

5. **Don't buy a fake ID.** Fake IDs are prevalent on college campuses, and they only promote bad behavior. If you can't wait until you're twenty-one, then you are asking for trouble. Also, if you get caught with a fake ID, the consequences from law enforcement are much worse.

6. **Take care of your friends.** If you're friends decide to drink and drink too much, take care of them. Make sure they stay hydrated and get home safe.

7. **Know what's in your cup.** If you drink, be wary of "PJ" and other mixed beverages.

Being different is hard, if you let it be. For nearly three years of my college career, I was the different one. I found other things to do on the weekends like going out to eat, watching movies, traveling to new places, and attending sporting events. I enjoyed each of my four years in college, and the drinking didn't affect my long-term happiness.

The short-term happiness of getting drunk and acting crazy isn't worth it in the long-run. Also, where does partying go on your resume?

CHAPTER 19

INTRAMURALS AND CLUBS

"EVERY DAY IS A NEW DAY FOR SOMETHING UNIQUE."

One of my favorite aspects of college is the availability of clubs, organizations, and intramurals that students can join. You can literally walk out of your dorm, apartment, or house on any given day and do something brand new. You can join a different club, play a different sport (without skill), and explore areas of interest. Socially, these activities allow you to grow outside of the classroom and the party scene; they allow you to socialize on a very unique stage.

If you're going to college, I'll assume that you were somewhat active in clubs, sports, or outside organizations in high school. I want to encourage you to carry those passions forward for a number of reasons:

- **College is a platform for you to try out your passions**. If you think you want to be a teacher, volunteer to teach. If you're interested in scuba diving, join the scuba club. I could go on and on. Clubs and organizations are fail-free activities. If you don't like them, find something else. It's that simple.

- **Freshman year sets the stage for years to come**. I WANT TO SCREAM THIS. Get involved as soon as you get to school – the day you move in, the day you set foot on campus. The more you get involved, the better chance you have to **Make the Most** of your college experience.

- **Intramural sports build friendships that will last a lifetime**. Regardless of whether or not you are athletic, if you've never played the sport, or don't understand the rules, get out there. I had the most fun running around on fields, courts, and playing sports I had no business playing. My senior year teams (basketball, flag football, and volleyball) held some of my closest friends that I will forever cherish.

  The size of the university you attend will dictate the number of clubs, organizations, and intramurals that are offered. UNC-Chapel Hill had so many clubs and organizations that I couldn't keep count. UNC had so many intramural sports that they even had made-up sports like "inner tube water polo." Simply put, if I didn't get involved in college, it was my fault. I can't say that every college has as many clubs as UNC-CH did, but I know that every college has the perfect organization for every student.

- **Try everything. Literally, try everything.** I spoke before about having balance in college, but as a first-year student, for a short period of time, you should try everything you can get your hands on. During my first year, I did so many random outside-of-the-classroom activities that I had to log them all down to remember.

1. **I joined the marketing club**. I thought I wanted to have a career in marketing, so I competed in a marketing-case competition. That didn't last long.

2. **I tried out for the cheerleading team**. To this day I still don't know why I tried out for the team. I think they wooed me by telling me that I looked athletic. They boosted my ego only to nearly kill me and a female cheerleader during my first and last practice. I lifted a cheerleader in the air only to drop her. Luckily, six other experienced team members were around me to catch her. Ironically, I became friends with the girl I dropped.

3. **I joined a variety of different Christian organizations on campus,** including Cru, which offered a large group worship every Thursday night. I was involved with Cru for a majority of my college career, regrettably never as much as I wanted to be.

4. **I tried out for the UNC JV basketball team**. As you remember, I eventually became a manager for the team, so you know I wasn't good enough to make it. However, I got to play my favorite sport in front of Roy Williams, one of college basketball's best coaches.

5. **I created and joined numerous intramural sporting teams**. Intramurals allowed me to be competitive (if I wanted to be, which most times I did), create funny names for teams, and compete for T-shirts. If you win an intramural championship at UNC-CH, you win a T-shirt. Luckily, I got to snag three championship T's in my time in college, and I still rock them with pride.

6. **I became a tour guide on campus**. This was by far the most enjoyable organization I was involved with. Every tour made me feel like I was a freshman again,

and I got to share my love of college with students like you! This was the one club that I stayed with from freshman to senior year. Not going to lie, my last tour was emotional for me.

7. **I was on a "paint-up" team that attended every home football game painted in Carolina blue body paint.** All of these activities were special to me, but there's just something about getting up early and painting your body for a sporting event that stands out above the rest.

At first glance, you might see that list as overwhelming, like I did too much during my first year. However, during that time I felt like I was **Making the Most** of every second. I was staying busy and having the time of my life. Your first year is much different than the rest of your college career. After trying everything I realized what I enjoyed and what I didn't. I stayed involved with the clubs that I enjoyed the most and focused on those.

Getting involved might mean something totally different than it did for me, but you HAVE to get involved. Try everything! Really, do it—because the worst thing that could happen is that you don't like something.

College is unique. College is new. Heck, college is unique and new every single day. Wake up every morning with a smile on your face and I promise you that you will **Make the Most** of every second while in college.

CHAPTER 20

SPORTING EVENTS

"GET HYPE."

As I mentioned in previous chapters, there are plenty of ways to **Make the Most** of your social life in college. However, no club, organization, or party gave me the same satisfaction as attending a sporting event in college with some of my closest friends. My fondest memories come from watching and cheering on our team, the Tar Heels. There's just something about gathering with thousands of students your age, getting hype, yelling, screaming, and celebrating a big victory.

I have countless stories that I could share about my time cheering for the Tar Heels, but none more exciting than the time I made the big screen (ESPN Top 10 play).

As soon as my alarm sounded on that Saturday morning during my freshman year, I felt an adrenaline rush, or it could have been the energy shot I quickly downed. I got up super early because the group I "painted up" with liked to be the first ones through the gates. The leader of our paint-up crew told me that being the first ones in the gate gives was infatuated with the idea of getting on TV during sporting events, and I quickly found out that camera men love painted-up students!

The game started off with two very impressive drives by our Heels, making the score 15-0 against the NC State Wolfpack. The Tar Pit (the student section) loved every minute of it. We were yelling, chanting, and dancing every time UNC trotted into the end zone. It was a very exciting game to watch. There was lots of scoring and it seemed like the game would never end. That was until Giovani Bernard (Gio) made one of the most iconic plays in UNC football history.

The score was deadlocked at 35-35 near the end of the fourth quarter, and everyone assumed the game was going into overtime. NC State failed to convert on third down, so they had to punt to Giovani Bernard.

Gio caught the ball, and the rest is history. Bernard jolted down the field, found a gap, and went alllllll theeeee wayyyyy! Bernard, filled with excitement, continued to run right at us on the front row. He jumped on the wall right in front of us. It was an incredible experience. People were smacking, screaming, and going berserk. I didn't think the excitement was ever going to die. In the process of all of the craziness, my sunglasses were slung onto the field, and I was punched in the lip. At the moment, I didn't even feel myself get hit, I was too wrapped up in the game, the excitement, and truly feeling like a student of the university.

The Tar Heels went on to win the game 43-35 in stunning fashion. It was an experience that I will never forget. Before the game, I decided to wear an orange hat (UNC's colors are Carolina blue and white) so that my mom could see me on TV if there was an opportunity. Luckily for me, I was featured on ESPN's Top 10 the next morning because of Bernard's "Carolina Leap."

Google Giovanni Bernard punt return *and you'll see a skinnier me in a bright orange hat when he jumps into the crowd.*

College gives you the platform to cheer and be a part of the team. It allows you to view so many different sports and support your classmates. I had friends who weren't even real fans of the game that loved cheering on the Tar Heels. I'm telling you, get involved with sporting events and go cheer on your team, whether that's lacrosse, soccer, volleyball, or fencing.

Not all of my college sporting event memories are positive. Some were truly quite depressing. If you're a big college basketball fan, then you know exactly what I am talking about.

I was a senior during UNC's 2016 National Championship run in basketball. The game ended in historic fashion and might go down as one of the greatest college basketball games of all-time. Kris Jenkins of Villanova hit a buzzer-beater to win the national championship, and as Villanova fans celebrated in Pennsylvania, we mourned in North Carolina.

I loved attending college sporting events. I waited in lines in the freezing cold, the snow, heck, I drove all across the East Coast cheering on the Tar Heels. No matter what college you attend, no matter how heartbreaking the losses, cheering on your team with your friends and fellow students is something I highly recommend.

CHEER LOUD, PAINT UP, AND SAY CHEESE

1. Wait in lines, especially for the big games.
2. Go all in. Cheer for all the teams; don't just be a football or basketball fan.
3. Attend sporting events with your friends.
4. Get hype and scream way too loud.
5. Make friends with the camera guy and maybe you'll find yourself on ESPN!

CHAPTER 21

GREEK LIFE

"THROW WHAT YOU KNOW."

Are you going to rush?"

Am I going to what?

When you first arrive to your college campus, that's a question you will often hear. The term rush means pledging a fraternity (frat) or a sorority (srat). Some of you might have parents who were in a frat or a srat, so you might have a little more knowledge than most, but I am going to explain to you what they are and the pros and cons of joining.

Frats/Srats are a collection of students that join the same brotherhood or sisterhood because of a shared interest or background. The two main types of Greek life are social or professional frats or srats. Social Greek life is the most common, and if you have ever seen big houses on college campuses with Greek lettering attached, these are the groups that occupy these houses. Professional fraternities are built around a group of students (male or female) who have the same career interests.

When I began college, I told my parents that I was going to join a fraternity. My dad quickly told me that if

I wanted to do that, I would have to pay for it. At first I was okay with that, but then I took a quick look at the cost and decided it was best to save my money for other things. Looking back, I realized that I was researching the most expensive fraternities to join, and if I would have been more passionate about joining, I would have found that there were much more affordable options.

Even though I never joined a fraternity (I'm not a female so I couldn't join a sorority), I had a lot of friends that did join. My friends, like most students, all joined for different reasons. Some joined to get more involved on campus, some to meet more people, and some needed something to add to their resume. During my time in college, I saw a lot of positives come out of sororities/fraternities, but I also saw some negatives. Joining for the wrong reasons can make these negatives come to life and are where some of these negative stereotypes concerning Greek life are born.

PROS OF JOINING A FRAT/SRAT

- As a member, you have instant access to people who have the same interests as you. In some instances, you also have access an extensive alumni network that you can reach out to for advice and mentorship.
- They have really awesome events. During my time in college, I was able to attend cocktails, formals, and different parties with my friends. They're usually themed based and are a fun way to end a week.
- Lifelong friends can be made, which is true for all parts of college, but members of frats/srats spend a lot more time together at events the organization may have.
- The final piece is more geared toward sororities (and a few fraternities)—they have cool hand signals that students love to post on social media. If you join a

sorority (ladies), you will quickly know what I am talking about. They'll often say "throw what you know" and members will throw up their hand sign for a picture.

CONS OF JOINING

- It's an additional cost on top of your tuition. Each organization has different cost levels, and this is the main reason I didn't join during my first year.
- Hazing can exist among certain frats, sometimes srats as well. Hazing can happen in a number of different ways, but the most common is making a pledge (someone who is joining the frat) drink too much alcohol. However, universities are very proactive in making sure that students are not hazed and are treated in a respectful manner.
- Students might get stuck only hanging out with members of their frat/srat. This isn't a terrible thing, but in order to **Make the Most** of your college career, you need to hang out with all types of people to get the best experience.
- Cheap beer. I don't enjoy cheap beer. If you join, you'll learn that cheap beer is a staple among fraternity parties.

Joining a frat/srat is totally up to you. It's a personal choice that you will have to make. I believe that is great for some people, but others, like myself, just didn't need it. It allows students to blossom socially and might give them an extra bit of confidence that they didn't have in high school. However, I don't believe you have to join a frat/srat to **Make the Most** of your social life in college.

PART 4

MAKE THE MOST OF YOUR OPPORTUNITIES

"YOUR NEW CHAPTER BEGINS ON MOVE IN DAY!"

It's no accident that this is the final section of the book—pay close attention to the following chapters because they will truly help you on your journey to **Make the Most** of your college career.

The day you move in is the first day of your new chapter. "New chapter?" you might ask. No matter where you came from, no matter what you did in high school, no matter the wealth of your parents, college is a time to start fresh. College gives you a clean slate with brand new opportunities, and the only person stopping you from going out there and grabbing them is you.

My favorite part of college was the fact that I could walk out of my dorm and find endless possibilities. On top of meeting a new person every day, I could try a different activity or club, I could start a business, learn about studying abroad, or get an on-campus job. Simply put, there's an endless amount of opportunities right outside of your dorm room. If you're not already excited to go to college by this point, I hope this gets your heart beating a little bit faster.

Come to college hungry for new experiences.

Coming from a small town made me eager for opportunities. I'm not saying that city folks won't be hungry for new adventures, but you have to realize that a town of 4,500 people doesn't have much. College was exciting from beginning to end, but the feeling of showing up on a campus filled with opportunities gave me a freshman-year high that was indescribable.

The following chapters will go through some of the biggest opportunities you have to **Make the Most** of your college experience:

Entrepreneurship or Entrepredoership
You never know where a simple business
idea can lead you.

Networking
Communication is key in landing the right opportunity.

Interviews
Learning how to interview effectively
will set you apart.

Internships
We all need work experience.

Jobs
On-campus and post-grad jobs can be hard to come by,
but not with proper prep.

Service
Opportunities shouldn't always benefit you;
lend a hand.

Travel and Experiences
Use free time to travel and make memories that will
last a lifetime.

Mistakes
College isn't rosy. Learning how to turn mistakes into
opportunities is key.

At the end of my campus tours, I would always stress to pro-spective students that your resume, your job application, and your new chapter starts the day you move into your dorm room. College is about **Making the Most** of the resources that the campus has to offer, and lots of those resources spawn great opportunity.

I hope the following chapters pump you up, and give you the motivation to chase all the amazing opportunities that college has to offer.

CHAPTER 22

ENTREPRENEURSHIP OR ENTREPREDOERSHIP

"WATERMELONS, NOT CARS. GET IT?"

An entrepreneur can be defined as a person who manages a business or businesses and takes on more than normal financial risks in order to make the business run effectively. An entrepreneur has endless opportunities; they're not scared of anything. They can come from any background, they can have any passion, and they believe that the sky is the limit.

At the young age of seven, my parents' friends called me the "little entrepreneur."

The entrepreneurial bug bit me at a young age because I was eager to make a quarter. As a child I would save all of my Halloween candy and resell it back to fans at my sister's basketball games. 100 percent margin wasn't bad for my first gig.

For all of my entrepreneurs out there, you know that once the entrepreneurial bug bites you, the sky is the limit. I went on to start numerous small businesses: a bow and arrow business, Austin's Amazin' Car Wash, a movie production business, a T-shirt design venture, and I even bought and placed bubble gum machines in restaurants. My trend of starting super small businesses in my town of Valdese came to a halt when I headed to college, but my entrepreneurial spirit continued to thrive.

Coming to college was an adjustment in every aspect of my life. The academics, the friends, the extracurricular activities, everything was different. These differences allowed my eyes to be widened and I saw that this world held way more opportunities than I ever imagined. For example, when I started hanging out with more of the business students, I learned that it might be best if I went to work for a bank, consulting firm, or sales company right out of college. My friends were telling me how much these jobs paid, and I couldn't believe it!

"I could make how much coming out of college?" The numbers were staggering, and I was amazed of my earning potential. Simply put, college broadened my perspective tenfold in the first few months I was there.

College students all across the world struggle with one big question: "What do I want to do with the rest of my life?" Some might never answer the question, and during my first two years of college, I had no idea what my answer would be.

During a trip to London with my roommate, Nick, I was reintroduced to my true passion (yes, Nick, you can take credit here). During our two-week stay, we visited a place called Tesco. Tesco, which is similar to Target in the United States, has a partnership with a company called Waves. Tesco customers can have their car washed while they shop. Being that I had started a car wash company (Austin's Amazin' Car Wash) when I was twelve years old, I was infatuated with what I saw that day in the parking lot. I had never before seen a business like it, of that size, in the United States. The experience was like a cartoon episode where the light bulb suddenly comes on above a character's head.

Upon my arrival back to the States, and the start of my junior year, I began researching the wash-while-you-shop car washing business model. There was little competition for a business like Waves in the United Sates, and I was determined to make this a reality. After pitching the idea to one of my suitemates, Randy Short, I took the idea to a class, and my career trajectory, or "what I wanted to do with my life" was made very clear.

Before I go any further about the business and entre-preneurship, let's take another look at the word *entrepreneur*. According to the Oxford dictionary, an entrepreneur is "a person who organizes and operates a business or businesses, taking on greater than normal financial risks in order to do so." Financial risk? Was I really an entrepreneur? I didn't feel as if I was going to have to take a huge financial risk, especially since I didn't have any money to do so.

BECOME AN ENTREPREDOER

Too often I heard other students come up with a great business idea (so they said), but they never acted on it. They never attempted to get it started, they weren't willing to get their hands dirty, and they were afraid to fail. Don't be afraid—college is the best place to chase an innovative idea or business concept. The only way you fail is if you don't try. It's that simple.

During your college career, you'll take one or two classes that will open your eyes to new things, impact you in a certain way, or in my case, completely open the doors to so many opportunities. Business 500: Introduction to Entrepreneurship taught by Jim Kitchen, a serial entrepre-neur, reintroduced me to what it meant to be an *entrepredoer*.

The class taught us to follow *The Lean Startup (written by Eric Ries)* model, which simply means taking your business idea and testing it with real customers at the lowest possible cost. As a college student, you'll learn money doesn't come easy, so bootstrapping a business is essential.

After being introduced to a waterless car wash product by a friend, Randy and I changed our business to a waterless car wash for shopping centers. We decided to call ourselves Waterless Buddy's and began testing our product on friends' cars. We hired one of my friends from back home to do some design work, and he created an awesome logo, and another one of my friends from back home helped us make our first company swag (T-shirts).

Getting the swag gave us the energy to hit the ground running. In a matter of weeks, Randy and I had partnered with a local mall to host a one-week test market of our car wash service.

On November 16, 2014, Randy and I started our business in a mall parking lot a few miles from our campus. Selling a waterless car wash to an older gentleman in a bright yellow shirt at 7:00 p.m. in a parking lot is not the easiest sell. However, at the end of our week test market, we had successfully washed fifty-four cars, made over $900, hired our friends to help us, and gained a lot of interest in our company. The test was a success.

Waterless Buddy's became much more than just a one-week test market at the local mall. After hiring three of our other buddies (Tyler, Taylor, and Kealia), we washed two hundred plus more cars, traveled across the country pitching our waterless car wash concept through business competitions, and enjoyed the time we got to spend with one another. Oh yeah, and we bought more swag.

I felt as if every day was a learning experience with this opportunity. Waterless Buddy's was a game changer in my college career, and it eventually introduced me to my current boss. Below you'll find some funny and interesting lessons we learned along the way.

WATERLESS BUDDY'S TAUGHT ME

- How to sell anything with the right determination
- How to write a business plan
- How to pitch to business leaders, even if you listened to Taylor Swift before going onstage
- How to network effectively
- How to manage, and more importantly, how not to manage
- How friendships can be ruined so easily through a business decision, but with time can be healed
- How one opportunity can lead to a bigger opportunity
- Failure is all about perspective
- It's OK to let go
- Watermelons, not cars! Get it?

An entrepredoer is someone that chases their passion by creating, implementing, and DOING an innovative business concept with the least amount of financial risk. By pursuing a business idea in college I was able to open more doors to more opportunities than I could've ever imagined. You can choose: be an entrepreneur or an entrepredoer. Just DO!

CHAPTER 23

NETWORKING

"IT'S NOT WHO YOU KNOW, IT'S WHO KNOWS YOU ON A FAVORABLE BASIS."

As I have mentioned before, opportunities are endless on college campuses. Opportunities come in all shapes and sizes, and some take more work than others to gain. By learning how to effectively network, no opportunity will be unreachable.

The word network means to connect and speak with others (students/professors/potential employers) to exchange information (email/phone number/business card). Networking can be done in any setting: in the classroom, during an event, playing a sport, anywhere! People who are great networkers are always connected to what is going on around them.

If you haven't done so already, make a business card! Business cards make you stand out, especially when you meet someone for the first time who is older and perhaps more connected than yourself. There was one time in particular that carrying a business card paid off in my favor.

At the end of every campus tour, I would always hand out a business card that had my name, phone number, and a link to my blog. I encouraged students to reach out to me with any questions they had while applying to college. After a tour during my junior year, I was doing my usual passing out of cards when a parent stopped me. He said, "Here, I'll give you my card. I think I know someone who can help you out." To be honest, I didn't know how to handle the situation, so I shook his hand, stuck the card in my pocket, and darted to class.

The parent ended up being an executive with internship opportunities. I sent him a follow-up email soon after the tour. The email led to a thirty-minute call and an interview for an internship. Even though the internship didn't work out, I was thrilled to have the chance to connect with him and learn more about the opportunities they had. Like I said, networking opportunities can come from anywhere—you just have to be ready.

No matter your desired college major or field of study, you need to know how to **Make the Most** of your networking opportunities.

1. **Know the networking environment.** Different environments call for different ways to network. A basketball court or a gym probably isn't the best place to approach someone about an opportunity they may have. However, there are internship/job fairs and networking sessions that allow you to speak to people on a more intimate level.

2. **Practice your elevator speech.** For me, a lot of my networking was done around my startup, Waterless Buddy's. I would stand in front of my mirror in my dorm bathroom and rehearse the elevator speech. I was that obsessed about making it the best it could

be. My elevator speech was quick (twenty–thirty seconds) and it showed why I was so passionate about what I was doing.

I understand that not everyone will have a business in college, but it is still crucial to have an elevator speech ready. For example, if you are trying to get involved with a club or organization, it will be good to have an understanding of why you want to be involved and why you think you would be an important part of the program.

Ex) Hi! My name is Austin Helms and I am a junior majoring in business. I am super interested in being on a committee for Relay for Life because I have lost a lot of my family members to cancer. I am determined to help this organization raise more money for cancer research.

3. **Networking is a two-way street. Learn to listen.** A lot of the times when young college students network, they forget to listen. They are so excited about the opportunities that are in front of them that they fail to listen to the other party. I was subject to this, and not listening can cause you to miss out on bigger opportunities. When speaking to another person, be sure to listen to their story. They, too, are networking and might see an opportunity in you!

4. **Treat everyone as if they are the President of the United States.** This is one of my favorite pieces of advice. No matter who the person is, no matter what, treat them with respect. A misconception of networking is that you are always trying to meet the next big person. Networking is about getting to know people for who they are, and if for some reason they have an opportunity for you, then that's great. However,

opportunities aren't gained by disrespecting people. Treat everyone like they are Mr. or Mrs. President.

5. **Follow up after you meet.** I have mentioned this before, but it is so crucial. After meeting someone for the first time, send a follow-up email, letter, call, or some kind of communication to thank them for their time and to learn more about their opportunity.

The word networking can be overused and looked at in a negative way when people only network for their personal benefit. As a former college student, I know it's difficult to want to connect others when you're not that connected. However, if you meet someone that could really benefit from meeting one of your friends, connect them! Trust me, this will pay off and people will begin to connect you to others.

During my senior year, one of my professors gave me this advice, "It's not who you know; it's who knows you on a favorable basis." For instance, you want to be that kind of person that shows up positively in other people's conversations. Always be respectful while networking, and always look the other person in the eye. You never know if the person you are talking to could be the one to open the door to the next job or opportunity. **Make the Most** of every person you interact with, no matter who they are.

CHAPTER 24

INTERVIEWS

"HOW MANY GAS STATIONS ARE THERE IN THE US?"

Whether you know it or not, you have been interviewed before. Interviews come in all different formats. They can be as informal as a parent of a high school girlfriend/ boyfriend questioning you about your life or as sophisticated as a CEO asking business-related questions that could land you your first job. Interviews are a way for people to test you on a face-to-face level and can oftentimes be the make-or-break point for getting a job or internship.

HOW TO PREPARE FOR AN INTERVIEW

I. **Schedule the right time.** All interviews are different, and there is a chance that you could be the only person interviewing for a certain position. No matter the case, when you schedule the interview can be a huge key to your success. Schedule your interview at the beginning or end of the time period given.

Most of the time interviewers will give you a time window of when they will be giving interviews. Make sure that you choose one of the first or last slots. The reasoning behind this tactic is that people usually remember the first and last folks they see. If this is a big position, you will most likely be competing with a number of different folks. Interviews could last all day for the interviewer—you never want to schedule an interview around lunch time.

2. **Understand the opportunity in its entirety. If you are applying for a job/internship:** study the company's website, read articles about their recent news, and if possible research the interviewer. If given the name of the person who will be interviewing you, looking them up on LinkedIn is never a bad tactic, just make sure you don't act like you know too much about them.

    If you are applying to a program/scholarship: study the program or scholarship and know why you are a fit. Interviewers love when they interview someone who is knowledgeable about the topic. This shows that they are truly interested in the program.

3. **Mock interviews are recommended.** Colleges/universities have career centers that will give you mock interviews before your big day comes. Even if you feel super comfortable interviewing, you should take advantage of this opportunity. If for some reason you don't have time, ask one of your friends to interview you with sample questions!

There were times during my college career when I wasn't prepared for the situation at hand. As you know, when you're not prepared, you usually don't act in the correct manner and you very rarely have a positive experience. During the beginning of my senior year, I applied for an office assistant job to make some extra cash. However, I didn't really research the position in depth before taking the interview.

When I arrived, the staff member was excited to meet me and we began the working interview. Essentially, this is where you do tasks they assign, and they observe. I was asked to do very simple jobs: fill the fridge, tidy up around the office, and more hands-on tasks, like going through paperwork. After about five minutes I could tell I wasn't a fit for the position, but I continued working. Following the interview, I met with two more of the staff in the conference room for a formal discussion. I didn't know it then, but I was walking into one of the most awkward interview sessions I had ever experienced. One of the staff members, asked me as soon as I sat down, "Do you think you could see yourself doing this type of work ten hours per week?"

Being honest, I simply told them no and that I didn't think that I had time for the position. "OK, we're finished." There was a long awkward silence. I asked if I should go, and they showed me to the door.

A month after the interview I had a meeting with the head of the same office. I had a meeting to discuss Waterless Buddy's (she had been a great mentor to our team on previous occasions). To keep the story short, I was completely caught off guard when she relayed to me her anger and disappointment with the disrespect I had shown her team. After listening to the story from their perspective, I saw how flippant and disrespectful I had been. Although I certainly didn't mean to waste their time and be disrespectful, I was. It took a mentor to point it out to me. It's never a great feeling to know that you didn't treat someone the right way, and it hurts even more when someone you know was hurt because of your actions. Following the meeting, I sent letters of apology to each of the staff members that interviewed me because it was the right thing to do. This was a HUGE learning experience for my professional career.

Interview prep is key to having a successful interview, whether you get the job or not. By being prepared you align yourself to be more respectful, and in turn, to receive a better outcome. Learn from my mistake and prepare yourself!

After preparing for the interview comes the fun stuff.

HOW TO ROCK INTERVIEWS

On the goal list that I made when I was seventeen years old was: "Rock my first real interview." That goal was made a reality during my freshman year when I interviewed with the *Daily Tar Heel,* UNC's college newspaper.

1. **Be yourself.** I know that sounds cliché, but no interviewer wants a fake interview. Be who you are in an interview. This tip will save you long-term headache. If you don't fit the position, then you don't really need to be awarded the position. We all have our fit in this world, and you shouldn't have to change yourself during an interview to get that.

2. **Shake their hand, share your first and last name, and make eye contact.** The very first thing you should do when you walk into an interview is shake the interviewer(s) hand and introduce yourself. Introduce yourself with your first AND last name. This will feel weird at first, but get used to it—there are a thousand different Austins in the world. Make yourself stand out.

   Eye contact is so important. Looking someone in the eye tells them a few things. "This person respects me, they are interested in what I am saying, and they are confident." The ONLY time you shouldn't be giving the interviewer eye contact is if you are taking notes on something they are saying. Be sure to exit the interview the same way you entered, with a handshake and eye contact.

3. **Ask questions.** Most interviews nowadays are doing a reverse interview and will ask you what questions you have. If you have done ample research, this will come easy. Have a few questions jotted down to ask them during the interview.

4. **Find a way to standout.** When I applied to the Kenan-Flagler Business School, there were a number of different factors that affected my admittance to the program: a few essays, my college GPA, and an interview. I knew that my essays and GPA were my weaker pieces, so I knew I had to rock the interview.

Since I had done a lot of entrepreneurial activities as a young child and through high school, I decided to bring some props with me to the interview. It wasn't required, but I wanted to show off my work. I brought a car washing hat, a T-shirt I had designed and sold, a spreadsheet filled with numbers from my small vending machine business, and a few pictures. This simple effort of going the extra mile is what I believe got me over the hump of getting into the business school.

5. **Dress to impress, but that doesn't mean buy an expensive suit**. Different interviews call for different dress codes. Make sure you look up the dress code before going to the interview, and if you are in doubt, wear a suit and tie.

When purchasing your first suit, you don't need to get anything fancy. A good suit can be purchased for around $99.

The only way for you to get better and feel more confident with interviewing is to be interviewed. Be sure and practice as much as you can before your big day.

PREPARE FOR ANYTHING

The last thing I will leave you with is to prepare yourself for any question that the interviewer might ask. I have been asked a number of different questions during my interviews, such as:

- How many gas stations are there in the United States?
- If you had a magic wand, what would you do to change the program?
- Where do you see yourself in ten years?

These questions are never looking for a distinct answer, but they are looking for your creative mind to activate and for you not to say, "Oh, I don't know."

The more you prepare for interviews, the more likely you are to be confident when you sit down at your first interview.

Just in case you were wondering, according to the US Census of 2012, there were over 114,000 gas stations.

CHAPTER 25

INTERNSHIPS

"TIME TO TEST THE WATERS; DON'T WORRY ABOUT THE MONEY."

Internships are unique in a lot of ways. They allow you to take the knowledge you gain from the classroom and test it out in a real-world scenario. In most cases, students can learn more from their internship than they can in the classroom. This is because an internship allows a student to see if they are truly passionate about a career field of choice, gives them a platform to use their talents, and allows the student a sneak peek of what it's like to truly be out on their own in the workforce.

No matter what college you attend, searching for a summer internship is a necessity for most students. On rare occasions, students who plan on attending graduate school don't have to work an internship, but it's always a plus if you can add some experience to your resume. For some, the internship search can be stressful, long, and have you asking yourself, "What am I going to do this summer?"

Before jumping into my experience with internships, there are a few things you need to know:

1. **Internships can be completed during any year of your college journey.** Most students complete one or two internships during their sophomore and junior summers.

2. **Internships can be unpaid, paid, or can give you class credit.** It all just depends on the internship. In my situation, my parents weren't going to pay for my housing during my summer internship, so I had to find a paid internship.

3. **Internships can also be completed during the semester, but in my eyes that's more of a part-time job.** Internships fully immerse you into the job, and that's really hard to do being a full-time college student.

4. **Most colleges/universities have internship/job fairs during the fall and spring semesters.** This is a time where you can learn more about opportunities in your area and beyond. Internships are offered all across the United States and the world! A great place to test and practice your networking skills.

5. **Believe it or not, most companies are extremely excited to hire young college students**, so smile big when you have opportunities to impress an employer (networking).

6. **You can't fail.** Internships are meant for students who want to try a career field out. Part of the learning experience is about making mistakes, so don't worry if you mess up while on the job. Of course you can choose not to do your work or show up late, but don't be worried about messing up while you are on the job otherwise. If for some reason you don't like the internship, that's perfectly fine. Think about it

this way: would you rather try a career field out as an intern or move to a new city, take a full-time job, and completely hate the work you're doing?

7. **You can gain a full-time job from an internship.** Most companies hire interns in the hopes of recruiting you when you graduate. If you perform well enough, companies will offer you a full-time job. Last, but certainty not least: **Make the Most** of every second you have during your internship. There will be times during your internship that you will have the opportunity to network with individuals at senior/ executive levels in the company. **Make the Most** of this, and don't forget your business cards!

As mentioned before, internships are used as tests. For example, during my sophomore summer, I had dreams of working for a large corporation before I had actually done anything remotely close to working for a large corporation.

During my first internship, which was more like a shadowing opportunity, I learned quickly that big-city, big-office settings weren't my thing. The shadowing opportunity was unique because I was in London working for one of the largest banks. My roommate during my sophomore year, Nick, had a connection (his dad), who organized an incredible opportunity for both of us.

Although the opportunity was amazing, it didn't encourage me to continue pursuing my dream of working for a large corporation. Internships are the best way to introduce students to an industry while causing minimal financial harm to the individual.

Searching for an internship can seem difficult. Look back at your goals, hopes, and desires, and it should help clear things up a bit.

The best way to search for an internship is to first figure out what your interests are, and connect with your college counselors or professors for contacts and direction. For instance, are you particularly interested in a certain industry, such as marketing, sales, journalism, sports, education, or research? Once you find some interests you may have, you can then begin searching for companies that would allow you to explore that interest.

Whatever your passion, there is an internship/opportunity. Make sure to take advantage of your university's career resources. These could include internship fairs, job expos, and mock interviews.

If you are offered multiple internship opportunities, I suggest listing the opportunities side-by-side with pros and cons for each position. I have found this strategy to be helpful in many aspects in life. However, I realize that some opportunities will be almost equal, and it will be very difficult to decipher which is best. This is where the support system I mentioned earlier in the book can help give you clarity.

My most beneficial internship opportunity came during my junior year when I had the opportunity to work as an Entrepreneur in Residence at a small product investment company. The company, Bootstrap Advisors, specializes in investing in niche products. The products spanned from antiperspirant hand lotion to map magnets. My bosses weren't scared to sell anything.

My three-month internship allowed me to test my cold-calling and cold-selling skills as I was tasked with selling a few unique products. One of which was an accessory for a duvet cover. I didn't even know what a duvet was, so I had to the ask the owner of a high end linen store to show me. Naturally, I didn't make that sale.

Internships, especially like the unique one I had the opportunity to take on, teach you a lot about yourself. They show you what you are truly passionate about and can open doors that you would've never imagined. They are a time to test to see if this is the career field you would like to pursue, and not necessarily a time to make money. As a wise man once told me, "Learn as much as you can right now. The money will come with time."

If you don't gain anything from this chapter, know this: I still don't use a duvet or a duvet cover, but if you do, I know your solution.

CHAPTER 26

JOBS

"GET A JOB THAT YOU'RE EXCITED ABOUT."

Most students attend college for two reasons: they want to get a real-world job one day or they want to go to graduate school, which will eventually gain them a real-world job. Although most come to college knowing they want a job, most don't know what they want that job to be. The sad part is, some college students will accept a job following graduation just because it pays the most or that's what one of their family members does for a living. I will use this chapter to challenge you to look for a job that fits you, not your parents, but you!

Jobs are all around college campuses. There are jobs for current students that allow you to make a part-time income and subsidize tuition, and there are jobs that are waiting for students once they graduate. I will use this chapter to explain different jobs you could gain while on a college campus (different than internships), how I got a real-world post-grad job, and finally, I will share some of the negotiation tactics I learned and used in my college career.

BE EMPLOYED WHILE IN COLLEGE

1. **Financial Reasons:** If you are paying for some or all of your college, a part-time job while in college is essential.
2. **Building your resume:** Some students come to college with little work experience. With all of the jobs that college campuses have to offer, students can explore different jobs and build their resume rather quickly.
3. **Entertainment and socializing:** Jobs on college campuses can be fun and entertaining, especially when you get to work with some of your friends.

I understand that a part-time college job isn't a lifelong career, but they help students get their foot in the door, and it's another testing platform to try out different interests.

Getting a job on a college campus is easier than you might think. College jobs can range from being a referee for an intramural sport to being an assistant in the library. Most of these jobs are considered work-study jobs and vary depending on the size of the college you attend.

Some companies will even recruit college students. These positions are called student ambassadors. I had the opportunity to be an ambassador for two companies, one of which allowed me to give out free cookies to other college students. Who wouldn't love a job where people love you back?

By working multiple jobs while in college, I was able to build my resume, my network, and have a lot of fun. I worked a total of four part-time paid jobs and a few other unpaid positions. These experiences allowed me to make extra money while in school, and ultimately helped lead me to my first big-boy job.

First, I hope you remember that your search for your real-world job doesn't begin your senior year of college. It begins the day you move into your dorm. Even more important, you'll find the job for you when you find the job that aligns with your passion. Nothing explains that better than the crazy story behind how I landed my first job with the Griffin Brothers Companies.

As I mentioned before, Waterless Buddy's allowed my team to present at numerous business-plan competitions. During one of the competitions, I had the opportunity to pitch to my first real-world boss.

Following our ten-minute pitch, we participated in a question-and-answer session with a panel of judges. To this day, I still laugh at what Mike, my current boss, said. "I don't like your business, but I know a guy who owns a large car wash company in Charlotte, North Carolina." As soon as he made his comment, my entire team perked up because we knew the company he was speaking of, and it just happened to be the second largest car wash in the United States. We knew we had to go talk to him.

To keep a long story short, I took his business card, emailed him, and our relationship began. We met during spring semester of my junior year, and built a strong connection during the fall of my senior year before he offered me a positon as an entrepreneurial apprentice in Charlotte. I know you must be wondering what that even means. Griffin Brothers Companies has a program for aspiring entrepreneurs to work within their company on small projects, look for new entrepreneurial opportunities, and pitch new ideas for the business to explore.

Although I had other opportunities, like working in California at a startup, or running Waterless Buddy's, I decided the best option for me right out of college was to work for Mike and the Griffin Brothers. This opportunity wouldn't have been possible without the small jobs and opportunities I pursued while in college. If you **Make the Most** of your time in college, you truly never know where a small, simple opportunity can lead you!

CONSIDER THESE TIPS FOR REAL-WORLD JOBS

1. Apply to as many jobs as interest you. You don't want just one option
2. Start early. Applications for real-world jobs begin during the fall of your senior year. You hard workers out there can even secure a job during your summer internship.
3. Don't apply to positions for monetary purposes alone.
4. Consult your support team when you are trying to decide between job offers.

The final piece I will touch on in regards to jobs is negotiation strategies. Negotiation can be used for a number of things when searching, choosing, and deciding on your first job. For example, you can negotiate salary, location, and start dates.

I had the opportunity to take a negotiations class while in college and it helped me tremendously with my internship and job search/selection process. Although I am no expert on the topic, I will give you advice/tips on what helped me succeed in negotiations:

- **Always negotiate.** I understand that some offers can be very, very good offers, but always look at the offer and ask yourself, does this align with what I want 100 percent? If it doesn't, negotiate.

- **Anchoring bias is a real thing.** The first to offer is usually the first to win the negotiation. For example, if you are given an option to choose when you start your job, you should always suggest a date first. If you leave it up to your employer, then they will most likely win the negotiation.
- **Negotiate with precision.** This is most important if you are negotiating salary. When you receive your offer, you need to have a great reason for asking for a higher salary. Just throwing a number out to an employer will get you nowhere. A 10 percent increase isn't too much to ask for, but don't get crazy.
- **Be respectful.** This goes without saying. If you are negotiating with the employer, this means you are interested in working with the company. Be sure you don't burn any bridges during your negotiating.

It is my hope and desire that you take preparing and searching for a job seriously. Sometimes jobs don't come easily, and they take work, patience, and grit. I never would have thought that washing cars without water would lead me to an incredible opportunity, but I was proved wrong. There is a reason for everything that you are doing while in college. **Make the Most** of every little job/opportunity, and you will find yourself sitting in a good place during your senior year of college.

One final tip about job hunting —don't get discouraged by your friends and classmates getting jobs before you. We all have different paths and desires in this life. Some jobs hire earlier than others, some students might want to serve abroad, and some might have to wait a little longer to find a job. Be patient as you wait, and don't be discouraged by your friends. Cheer them on!

I came to college to find a real-world job, but not just any job. A job that I would love, be passionate about, and that would one day lead me to where I want to take my career. That job is out there for you—just go find it!

CHAPTER 27

SERVICE

"AUCTIONEER AUSTIN GETS A $20 BID"

While in college, stay grounded.

Quickly, you will learn how easy it is to become selfish. College isn't meant to make you selfish, but it makes you very independent. This independence can push you to make better grades, get involved with opportunities to boost your resume, and teach you how to live on your own. College can get busy with all that is going on, and sometimes it's hard not to think about yourself.

Although college makes it very easy to only focus on yourself, college also makes it very easy to serve other people. Serving other people can come in the way of raising money for a cause, helping kids, or starting a non-profit.

Every student is different in how they serve. For example, I have friends who were involved with an event called Dance Marathon (DM). DM raises money for the UNC Children's Hospital to provide emotional, medical, and financial support to the families. The event encourages the students involved to raise money throughout the year and is capped off with a night full of fun and excitement. The event itself is incredible: students stand for twenty-four hours straight to support and raise money for the organization. All of my friends who were involved said the end of the night is the best part. It's not the best part because they finally get to sit down after standing for over twenty-four hours, but because some of the children who they are impacting come to the event. Students shed tears of joy each year when the children come into the room, and it always helps remind the students that they are making a difference in these children's lives.

I was never a participant of Dance Marathon, but I saw how impactful it was in my friends' lives. Service in college can really change your perspective and give you a new outlook on life. Service also gives you a break from the competitive side of things. When it comes to serving others and making a difference, college students can come together to build something beautiful.

By staying busy in college, it made it hard for me to serve as much as I would have liked. However, I was as an admissions ambassador, which is a college tour guide, and had the chance to show off my auctioneer skills during my senior year to help raise money for a camp that benefits children who have parents with cancer, called Camp Kesem.

Becoming a tour guide and giving tours was one of my favorite things to do while in college. I enjoyed serving with the admissions office because I loved having an influence on future college students. That's another reason why I wrote this book, and why I am so passionate about you **Making the Most** of your college experience. Nothing made me happier than speaking to a bunch of excited high school juniors and seniors on a brisk fall afternoon in Chapel Hill.

I would usually get asked, "Do you actually like giving tours of our campus?" My answer was always the same, "Of course, it makes me feel like a freshman again!" The service I was involved with gave me new life. It energized me because I was feeding a passion. And looking back, college freshman really do have the best attitudes. I am beyond thankful for the opportunity I was given to serve as a tour guide.

No matter what you're passionate about, there is a place for you to serve while in college. There is no perfect college recipe to make sure that you **Make the Most** of every second, but I would say having the most well-rounded college career that you can have is a good start. Below, you'll find some tips on how I would start my search on getting involved on campus in the service sphere:

1. **Search for service oriented clubs/organizations on your college's website.** Most universities have a list of all clubs/organizations. If you know the area that you are passionate about, check out some related organizations. If your preliminary research gets you excited, email the chair/president of the organization. They are always excited to get more volunteers.

2. **Talk to friends, older students, or professors.** Your best resource on your college campus is the people. Talk to others, see what's offered and what they would recommend. You never know the opportunities that can spawn from conversation!

3. **Go for it!** If you want to really prepare for your college journey, I would make a list of organizations you are interested in and check them out as soon as you arrive on campus. Don't just talk about getting involved with serving an organization. Get out of that dorm room and go impact lives!

4. **Get out of your comfort zone.** Get way out of it. In my last stretch of college (second semester senior

year), I volunteered to be an auctioneer at a charity auction for Camp Kesem. Since I had no tie to the camp, I was a bit scared to volunteer, especially as something I was not (an auctioneer). Auctioneering is in my blood, though. My grandpa owns an auction company, and my cousin works for a big auction firm, but other than that, my only experience was joking around with friends selling fake items.

The auction I had volunteered for made it even funnier. It was a student-athlete date auction. The director of the camp had asked athletes from all across the school to volunteer themselves to go on dates with anyone who would pay the right price. These events are usually fun, and the athletes get a real kick out of who goes for the biggest price. Needless to say, the event made me nervous because I wasn't ready to talk "auctioneer fast" in front of one hundred people I didn't know.

As I took the stage, somehow all my nervousness went away. I explained the rules of auctions and how they were going to bid. The crowd enjoyed my corny jokes, and I started the first date at $15. "I got a fifteen-dollar bid; let me get a twenty-dollar bid!" I felt energy as the bids continued to climb for dates with the athletes. By the end of the night, we had raised almost $1000 for Camp Kesem. Stepping out of your comfort zone can not only help you grow, but can also make an impact in someone else's life.

Find a way to serve and stay balanced. I promise you that you'll **Make the Most** of your service opportunities while in college!

CHAPTER 28

TRAVEL AND EXPERIENCES

"THE BEST CLASSROOM DOESN'T HAVE FOUR WALLS"

On top of studying abroad, college can offer you free time to travel to new cities and experience things that you just can't experience on a college campus. Before arriving to college, I had never been north of Philadelphia, east of North Carolina, south of Florida, or west of Tennessee. Needless to say, college allowed me to break all of those travel barriers. I was able to travel to New York City and New Jersey on a mission trip, I went abroad to London and South Africa, and I had many trips out west to Dallas, Denver, Los Angeles, and San Francisco. One of the great parts about my travel in college was that I "balled on a budget." Most of these trips were either paid for/subsidized by the school or were very cheap! (Some of them required me to dip into my bubble gum machine fund).

The memories that I gained while traveling are endless. Having the ability to travel with some of my closest friends during college was one of my favorite things.

TRAVEL TO NEW PLACES

- Travel with friends and family. You'll make memories that'll last a lifetime.
- Take too many pictures.
- Visit other college campuses
- Go see where your friends live. This allowed me to go all over the US and the UK.
- "Ball on a budget." Travel cheaply by sharing gas and hotel costs.
- Make a music playlist. What's a road trip without a great playlist?
- Stay spontaneous.
- Say yes. If someone offers a free place to stay or free tickets, say yes.
- Be patient with your friends and family.
- Make plans for your next trip.

College gives you exposure to many different people, from many different places. This exposure made me take interest in traveling to new places. Below I'll highlight some of the unique stories that came from my travels.

London, UK (Sophomore)

Since I had never been out of the country, I had to buy a passport. If you don't have one—do it ASAP!

The trip was incredible, and I felt like I got to see everything that London had to offer and then some. I got to see Big Ben, the London Eye, Stonehenge (outside of London), and many more iconic attractions. *All are must-sees if you ever have the opportunity!*

My hosts, the Kramers, were even more incredible. Luckily for me, my roommate's family allowed me to stay at their house for free and give me the best first-time-abroad experience that I could've hoped for. By the way, if you ever go to London, *please mind the gap*!

Atlanta and Louisville (Junior)

My trip to Atlanta and Louisville was one of the funniest trips I took while in college. The original plan for the trip was for part of the Waterless Buddy's team to compete in a business competition in Atlanta. On the way to and from we were going to stop by Lexington, North Carolina (home of T. Beck, a team member) and Valdese (my hometown, of course). However, as you quickly find out in college, plans can change in an instant. For this trip they changed for the better.

Following the business competition, T. Beck used his basketball-friend connection to score us free tickets at an away UNC basketball game in Louisville, Kentucky. We couldn't pass up the word free, so we made the trek to Louisville.

It was another incredible trip that made me realize if you want to truly get to know someone—take a road trip. During that trip we drove through seven states (and saw an eighth, Indiana) and made memories on the country roads of West Virginia that I will never forget.

Denver, Los Angeles, San Francisco (Senior Year)

During my last winter break of college, I decided to take a trip out west to visit Randy in Denver and Brett in Los Angeles. It also worked out perfectly to visit them because I scored an interview in San Francisco while I was en route. Again, I got to experience things in Denver, Los Angeles, and San Francisco that I had never seen before. I got to play in the snow in Denver, hike to the Hollywood sign, and interview for a startup company. College is incredible because college has cool friends in cool places!

When you begin traveling (if you haven't already), you will eventually have an unfriendly experience in an airport. While in route from Denver to LA, I had the great opportunity of sitting in the Denver airport for a whopping fifteen hours. The snow that I had thoroughly enjoyed a few days prior had delayed and canceled tons of flights. The airport wait made me practice patience on a level I had never experienced.

Traveling in college allows students to have very unique experiences that can't be found in the classroom. You must take the initiative to go and be spontaneous when the time comes.

CHASE YOUR OWN "OH MY" MOMENTS

During my time in college I was famous for saying the phrase "oh my!" I didn't realize how often I said the phrase until people pointed it out, but it's a phrase that I wanted to live my college experience by. If you're not saying "oh my" at least once a day, are you truly **Making the Most** of your opportunities? An "oh my" is used when I am wowed or amazed. College is truly amazing and you must fill your journey with "oh my" moments.

I never had more "oh my" experiences in a row than I did during spring break of my senior year. In a span of three days, I won a slot machine jackpot with my Granny Kat, kissed the girl who might one day become my wife, and went skydiving.

How you spend your free time in college is truly up to you. However, I know that if you spend your time traveling and having unbelievable experiences, your college experience will be a big "oh my."

CHAPTER 29

MISTAKES AND FAILURES

"FIND POSITIVITY IN THE NEGATIVITY."

Make no mistake, I failed in many ways during college. You can fail in the classroom, on the athletic field, with opportunities, relationships, jobs, you name it, failure looms everywhere. Failure can tear apart a college journey in a heartbeat, but in the same breath, it can turn a college journey around.

I want you to **Make the Most** of your mistakes while in college because they will happen. My high school basketball coach used to always tell the team, "You can always tell who the best players are on the floor because they are always calm in the storm. Rarely do you see a great player get phased." I want you to become that player, that college student, who no matter what, doesn't give up and stays calm in the storm.

When you graduate from high school, you will probably receive a lot of recognition from your relatives and loved ones. As you know I believe in a strong support group, so be sure to thank those people for their support over the years. It's likely that your support team and family will give you cards that will be shiny and tell you all the great things you are going to do in college. Sometimes these cards will have money, sometimes not, but they all will encourage you and make you feel like you're going to conquer college. They won't warn you about failure and how to act when you fail or make a mistake.

I'm not trying to scare you or make you feel like college will be overwhelming, but I am trying to prepare you for everything that college will throw at you.

Below you'll find some of the ways that I failed in college. I will also explain how I dealt with the situations.

EXAMS

I'm not talking to you young geniuses out there, but to you average folk. You will fail an exam or make a grade that you are not used to making in college. I was an all-A student in high school, and receiving a failing grade on an exam is a hard pill to swallow.

How I dealt with it

It's tough to see a failing grade, or a grade you're not used to making. However, it motivated me. It made me hungry to do better in the classroom and focus more. It encouraged me to go to office hours and reach out to the professor. That failing grade got me into shape very quickly.

As years progressed in my college journey, I learned that grades don't define you. You define you. Stress less on exams and work harder during the year, and those grades will be less shocking. Take it from a kid who nearly called his mom crying after a few exams.

JOBS

During the beginning of my sophomore year, I became a football manager. It's a job that's difficult to obtain because of the glamour of getting free athletic gear, free travel to games, and the perks of being an athlete without really being an athlete. Simply put, the job had awesome perks, but you had to put in the hours. A ton of hours.

Becoming a football manager was my first big failure in college. It became a failure because I quit after six days on the job. During those six days, I realized that I wasn't cut out for the job, that I didn't have it in me. It was a hard job that I greatly respected, but I had to walk away. However, walking away got me a lot of ridicule from the other managers, and it was a dark time during my college career. I felt as if I couldn't stand back up on my own feet.

Quitting a job with all those perks and free gear was difficult. Especially when I knew the ramifications would get me talked about behind my back. However, that failure didn't turn out as bad as I thought.

How I dealt with it

Since I quit the job at the beginning of my sophomore year, I had a lot of excess time that needed to be filled. I was determined to get back in the workforce, and I scored two jobs. I became an assistant at the alumni association doing basic office work, and I became a JV basketball manager. Neither of those opportunities would've come about if I wouldn't have failed.

I dealt with this failure by jumping back in. College will make you feel worthless at times. However, you must stay positive in the negative. No matter what people say about you, get back into the thick of things.

EXPERIENCES

As college gives you many fun experiences, like skydiving, it can also give you scary near-death experiences.

During one of my travel experiences to see a friend in Louisville, Kentucky I flipped a Polaris RZR. It's a high-powered four-wheeler that should only be driven by the experienced of drivers. Luckily, we left the wreck with only a few scratches. The wreck was my mistake. I was completely careless and flipped the RZR by driving out of control on wet grass.

How I dealt with it

The wreck totally shook me up and did so for quite some time. I learned that sometimes our mistakes can really catch us off guard and make us reevaluate ourselves. I dealt with this mistake by truly reflecting on how I went about living my life. Being reckless and irresponsible with someone else's vehicle is never a way you want to learn your lesson, especially when it could end your life or your friend's.

I failed in many more things in college, in opportunities I had, the way I treated relationships, and even how I communicated with individuals. Even though some of my mistakes seemed unbearable at the time, they were very useful for my growth.

LEARN FROM YOUR MISTAKES

1. College allows you to make more mistakes with less consequences. So it's OK. Move on and get back on your feet.
2. You will fail time and time again. It only matters what you do next.
3. Fail early! Learn from your mistakes and don't do them again.

It might sound odd, but you truly can **Make the Most** of your mistakes and failures while in college. They help mold you into the person you will become. My Aunt Tina was a prime believer that each day is a new day, and you should always find positivity in the negativity.

CHAPTER 30

MAKE THE MOST

"IT'S THAT SIMPLE."

You'll wake up one day and you'll be in college. You'll blink and you'll be a senior, and before long, college will be in your rearview mirror. It is so important that each day you **Make the Most** of it.

I hope that through this book, you were able to gain insight on what it means to **Make the Most** of yourself, your academic life, your social life, and your opportunities while in college. I also hope that this book will lead you to your graduation, and when you look back at it all, you'll reminisce on what it took to get you there.

Following my graduation, my mom, her best friend, Gretchen, and my father threw me a graduation party. The party couldn't have been better. It wasn't the food or the cake that made it so memorable, but the people that surrounded me. I knew it was a special time when my kindergarten teacher walked in the room. I stopped what I was doing and greeted her with a hug. I remember thinking, "Wow, this journey started seventeen years ago in a little town, in a little school, with a little boy." Now, the tables were turned. I was much taller than her, but I still felt like that little kindergartener. It was a special moment.

"I graduated college," I said out loud as I stood outside my house after the party. In fact, I was standing in the same spot that I took a picture four years before. That picture was with my cousin, Brianna, and it was at my high school graduation party. Funny how things happen.

College is a place with lots of chapters, ups and downs, opportunities, and failures. It truly has it all. It tests you in the classroom, in the social scene, and spiritually. I **Made the Most** out of my college experience, and for that reason, I have no regrets as a college graduate.

When I think back to the day I moved into college, I remember being excited, ready to begin again, and to find new opportunities. Now, I am just a guy **Making the Most** of my real-word life. It's a little bit different than the flair of college, but I am **Making the Most** of every moment.

Wherever you are, wherever you come from, or wherever you may end up going to school, know that college has endless possibilities and it's built for you to **Make the Most of Your College Experience!**

FINAL THOUGHTS

Before you arrive on campus, here are some things you might need to know or do:

Packing

It's always better to have it and not need it than to need it and not have it. Before packing I would make a detailed list including the following:

- Clothing: If you're going to a college that is far away from home (like a plane ride away), I would pack all of your clothing (fall/winter/spring).
- Toiletries: Make sure to pack your deodorant!
- Entertainment: If you play an instrument or sport, be sure to bring your gear with you.
- Cleaning materials: Most universities will have cleaning taken care of, but you'll need to keep your room clean. Your level of cleanliness will determine the amount of cleaning supplies you want to bring.
- Bedding: If you're staying in a dorm during your first year, be sure to get the XL twin sheets!
- Check your school's housing page for a more detailed list, but this will get you started!

Saying Good-byes

One of the hardest parts about moving to college is saying your good-byes. This can be tough for some students, others not so much. However, I encourage you to go and see the family members and friends that mean the most to you and tell them how much you love them. Also, don't forget that they are always just a phone call away!

Relax

Have fun and relax during your summer before college. Lots of students will travel, read, or just sit by a pool. Find time to just chill.

New Hobbies

With free time before college, find a new hobby. Learn a new sport, learn how to code, or just do something completely different!

New Roommates

One of the most beneficial things I did before moving into college was meeting up with my roommate. If your random roommate is close enough for you to meet up, I would strongly advise you do so. If meeting up isn't an option, be sure to schedule a FaceTime or Skype meeting!

Orientation

When upcoming college students think of college orientation, they usually think of a ton of boring meetings. Well, I am here to tell you that there are a ton of meetings, but what you do with the meetings is up to you. Orientation gives you the opportunity to meet new friends, and it's the beginning of your college journey. Although the meetings might seem boring, be excited to be there and **Make the Most** of the time at orientation. I am still very close friends with some of the people I met during orientation.

Personal Time Capsules

How awesome would it have been if you could have seen a video of your parents when they were your age? Maybe you have a video, but I sure don't and I wish I did. So I decided to make a video of myself as a graduated high school student. In the video I spoke of my dreams, my goals, and my current life as it was. I videoed my house, my room, and the car that I drove in hopes that one day I could look back on it and show my kids how life used to be. I also did this to make sure I keep my goals and dreams intact. If you don't own a video camera, write a letter to yourself or take pictures of your house. Do something that will capture your memories.

Goals

Get started today! Set goals early and often! It's incredible how my goals changed from precollege to post-graduation!

Moving In

Your final steps before college will be filled with excitement and anticipation. Be sure to know when you will be permitted to move into your dorm. All colleges do move-in differently, and although the process can be stressful, it's an exciting time. Be ready!

Read and Share

Thank you again for picking up my book and making it to the end! Be sure to continue reading different books that challenge your way of thinking. Share my book with your friends, or anyone that you believe could benefit from my book! There is also a section of my website where you can post questions, goals, and your own insights. I look forward to hearing from you soon!

AUSTIN'S **TOP 16** LIST:

HOW TO BE
SUCCESSFUL IN COLLEGE

BECAUSE I HAD TO GIVE A SHOUT-OUT
TO ALL THE 2016 GRADS)

1. **Make the Most** of your college experience. **Make the Most** of every second. **Make the Most** of your friendships. Time in college flies by, don't waste a second.
2. Try everything possible. College is a testing ground; failure isn't really failure when you learn something. Get out there and try it all.
3. Love your school! I can't say this enough. Show your school spirit every time you get a chance.
4. Start now! Your resume, job application, and next chapter begins the day you move into college.
5. Become a doer. Do things in college; don't talk about doing them.
6. Stay balanced. An unbalanced college career can be disastrous.
7. Pray continuously and have faith.

8. Grades are grades. Don't fret over a bad grade. It happens.
9. Play intramurals, even if you're not athletic.
10. Study abroad and travel when possible!
11. Serve your college community! We all have our place to serve. Find that place early in your career.
12. Explore entrepreneurship. Remember, you don't have to be a business student to be bitten by the entrepreneurial bug.
13. Find your passion by exploring unknown territories.
14. Be proud of where you come from. Valdese, North Carolina!
15. Make goals, revise goals, make more goals, and then act on those goals! *(Email me with your goal lists!)*
16. Reflect on your experience by blogging, talking to friends, and debriefing with your support group!

ACKNOWLEDGMENTS

When I began writing this section of my book, I quickly realized that there are a ton of people who have made a lasting impact on my life. This book wouldn't have been possible without my family, friends, teachers, professors, and mentors. With that being said, I won't bore you with a long list of names, those folks just know I owe them a big hug.

During my Business Improvisation class each student was tasked with giving a sixty-second speech. The speech couldn't be rehearsed, and our professor encouraged us to speak about something that we were passionate about. Two of my classmates' speeches really hit home: "Anyone can be sad—it takes effort to be positive—make that effort." and "You never know what people are going through; always give them your best." After hearing those two speeches, I was motivated to continue to live a positive lifestyle.

Be thankful, be positive, be the same to everyone. Relationships are so important, and you never know the impact you can make on someone's life. Thank you again to all who has left a lasting impression on my life, college wouldn't have been the same without you!

ABOUT THE AUTHOR

Austin Helms is an entrepredoer and project manager in Charlotte, North Carolina. He is a proud graduate from the University of North Carolina's Kenan-Flagler Business School. Austin is passionate about seeing other college students succeed. If he's not speaking to students about college or starting a business, you might find him playing  country songs on his guitar, swinging a tennis racket, or playing basketball in a gym filled with hoopers.

If you would like to contact Austin, give him a call or shoot him a text (828-448-5521).

Reach out today, don't wait!

Austin Helms
(828) 448-5521
austinhelms32@gmail.com
austinhelms.org

Made in the USA
San Bernardino, CA
28 June 2017